Keeping
a Horse
Outdoors

KEEPING
A HORSE
OUTDOORS

Susan McBane

David & Charles

To my parents and family
for the good things in my life

Other titles in *The Equestrian Library* series:

THE HORSE OWNER'S HANDBOOK
Monty Mortimer

THE HORSE RIDER'S HANDBOOK
Monty Mortimer

LUNGEING
Sheila Inderwick

A DAVID & CHARLES BOOK

First published in the UK in 1984
Reprinted 1985
Revised edition published 1992
First published in paperback 2003

Distributed in North America
by F&W Publications, Inc.
4700 East Galbraith Road
Cincinnati, OH 45236
1-800-289-0963

ISBN 0 7153 1593 5

Line illustrations by Ray Hutchins

Printed in Great Britain by Antony Rowe Ltd.
for David & Charles
Brunel House   Newton Abbot   Devon

Visit our website at www.davidandcharles.co.uk

David & Charles books are available from all good bookshops;
alternatively you can contact our Orderline on (0)1626 334555 or write to us at
FREEPOST EX2 110, David & Charles Direct, Newton Abbot, TQ12 4ZZ
(no stamp required UK mainland).

Contents

1 First Things First

To a horse-lover, surely one of the most relaxing and pleasing sights anywhere is that of horses grazing peacefully in lush, green pastures with shady trees and crystal clear water gurgling nearby. Imagine a soft, balmy day in late spring, the sunshine warm on our backs as we lean over a gate taking in the restful scene. The flies have not yet become bothersome, and the only sounds we hear above the usual summer music of birds chirping and bees buzzing are those of the horses rhythmically cropping and chomping the grass, and the whirr of a distant tractor bringing with it on the light breeze the heady scent of new mown hay.

The grass is at its best, the horses are well fed, sleek and comfortable; everything is right with their world. These are undeniably the perfect conditions for an outdoor life. Worries such as mud fever, sodden ground, bitter winds and incessant rain, or, in summer, inflamed eyes from the flies, hard ground, jarred legs and broken feet, all seem far away.

But for how long do these ideal conditions last? A month, maybe? Two at the most, and then all the old, familiar problems start creeping back as spring turns to high summer and the year wears on. There is some respite in autumn, but winter takes over all too soon.

Advantages and disadvantages

People keep horses at grass for various reasons, the most common being lack of facilities and/or time to care properly for a stabled horse. Other reasons include the need to give a horse a period of rest and relaxation after a season's hard work, or to economise on food and bedding which can both be replaced by grass during the warmer times of year. Breeding stock and youngsters spend most of their time at grass not only for ease of management but because a great

deal of natural exercise and fresh air is vital to the correct
mental and physical development of a young animal, and the
health and development of a broodmare and her unborn foal.

From the human point of view, the good points about this
system of horse keeping are that it is less tying, the horse will
feed, water and exercise himself as he wishes and money can
be saved if the pasture is adequate. There is no thorough,
energetic grooming required, no desperate need to exercise
the horse if one has no time, and not such a strict timetable
to adhere to as regards feeds and general routine.

But although keeping a horse entirely at grass does not
take up so much time and money as keeping one stabled, it is
not a cheap trouble-free way of horse maintenance if one is to
keep the animal in a healthy, happy state.

The first problem may be finding a suitable convenient
field. A cramped, exposed, marshy, starved patch of land is
worse than useless for a horse out all the time, as is a rich,
lush cattle pasture. There is no stable to muck out, but droppings will have to be picked up daily from the shelter shed
(which is essential for a horse out for long periods), and if the
pasture is restricted or over-stocked the droppings will need
picking up from the grass regularly, too, in the interests of
good grassland management.

The horse will still need grooming lightly and examining
as regards condition, wounds, injuries and signs of ill-health
or other disorders. A grass-kept animal can never be as clean
and fit as one kept largely stabled; he could be very wet and
dirty when caught up to be worked - if he allows himself to be
caught at all and tending and handling a horse outdoors can
be difficult and unpleasant in bad weather.

Most owners will probably have a twice daily journey to
and from the (possibly rented) field in all weathers, and if the
field is some distance from one's home there is the regular
bother of transporting hay, concentrates, tack and other
necessities, unless secure storage is available nearby.

The horse might need extra food at least once a day, and
his water supply checking along with fencing and gates, and
an eye will have to be kept on other sources of danger such as
litter thrown or blown into the field and poisonous plants

developing. Tack, headcollars and New Zealand rugs will still have to be cleaned, rent found, worming medicines bought and the feed merchant, veterinary surgeon and farrier paid for normal maintenance work, as well as emergencies.

A major disadvantage which has arisen over the past few years is the risk of your horse being stolen for the meat trade. Rustling is now rife in Britain and it causes great distress not only to the owners but to the horses, too, who are subjected often to long and repeated journeys in rough waggons crammed with other unfortunates who trample on, kick and bite one another in their panic. Horses, ponies, donkeys, broodmares with foals and also stallions are herded indiscriminately together and hawked from sale to sale until sold, often injured and seriously run down, to the knackerman. Once a horse is sold through a public auction, his owner cannot get him back other than by buying him from the person who bought him there. Some horses, however, are not stolen for meat but simply for joy riding. Some have been ridden to death and others killed by traffic after being released on to a road.

Other considerations from the horse's point of view are just as varied. On the credit side is his obvious freedom to move about as he wishes and to eat to his heart's content. He has full and natural physical and social contact with his friends and the odd skirmish or two simply add interest to life, provided they are not serious. Horses are often happier and healthier when living a properly arranged outdoor life.

Unfortunately, for most of the year there are as many disadvantages as advantages, particularly if the horse is left too much to his own devices. In summer, the worst problem is flies and I believe most people do not realise (or, in some cases, turn a blind eye to) the immense misery these pests often cause. From late summer on, the food value of the grass starts to decrease until, by late autumn, it is worth practically nothing, resulting in an increasingly thin and hungry horse. Then the cold, wet weather comes, accompanied very often by winds of varying severity, not to mention frost, sleet and slushy mud; if the horse has inadequate shelter and food, he is going to start suffering considerably. Notwithstanding shelter, wet conditions are the contributing cause of the painful and common condition known as mud fever, and its allied complaint, rain rash or rain scald.

The right horse for the job

Correct, humane management can greatly diminish many of the problems but, even so, not every horse is a suitable candidate for living out. Although the worst prospects are the thin-skinned, hot-blooded, sensitive Thoroughbred, Anglo-Arab and Arab types and the best any of the hardy, heavy types such as native pony, cob and heavy horse and their crosses (others falling somewhere in between), even within these different types there are individuals showing varying constitutions and preferences. Thus, we may have a half-bred horse who curls up at the first sign of wind or rain or, conversely, an Arab who grazes happily in all but a blizzard, or a Shire who gets mud fever as easily as a white-legged, chestnut Thoroughbred. Much depends on the individual, who must be closely assessed by the person responsible for his care.

The breeding of the horse can be taken only as a broad guide. Some individuals do not have the physical resistance essential for a life of more or less exposure. Intimate observation and knowledge of the particular horse, culminating in an honest opinion as to the horse's suitability for outdoor living, is the only way to decide whether he can thrive and be happy on this system of management.

Basic necessities for the outdoor life

The first essential is obviously a field. This must be well drained or for at least six months of the year it will be out of use because of squelching mud or waterlogging. Wet land cannot support a healthy and abundant growth of the right kinds of grasses for feeding horses and, as mentioned, favours the development of mud fever and also foot rot. If poor drainage is combined with a heavy, sticky soil or clay, the problems will be even worse. Also unsuitable is land

An ideal field, with thick hedges and spreading trees which provide shelter. Company is also important, and even if the horses cannot share the same field, they can communicate over the fence if discretion is exercised over suitable neighbours. The post and rail fencing has had an extra bar run along the 'wrong' side to protect horses who may knock against the square posts. Two-rail fencing is adequate for adult horses, and cheaper than three-or four-rail fencing

which bakes hard or cracks in hot, dry spells, such as, again, clay. This can cause not only poor grass growth but jarring to the legs and feet, plus broken hooves in some cases, especially when flies are bad and horses gallop frequently to escape them.

There must be a healthy growth of nutritious but not over-rich grass to provide food, with no poisonous plants or trees within reach of the horses. The fencing must be safe, strong and high enough, as must the gates. There must be a generous, clean water supply, either natural or provided by the owner, and truly effective shelter at all times of year. General safety must be considered, such as whether there are any pits, dykes or unsafe ponds within reach, any farm implements or litter left in the field or dangerous hazards like concealed tree stumps and rabbit holes. It is worth considering, too, the field's proximity to any residential area which might be the source of vandalism, such as the joy riding already mentioned, razor-slashing, releasing on to the roads or other harassment.

Another important point, dealt with more fully later in the next chapter, and one frequently overlooked by owners, is that the horse must have a companion if he is to be truly content, otherwise he will probably not thrive or will constantly hurt himself trying to get out of the field in search of a friend.

Finally, there is the nature of the human attention available to the horse. Knowledgeable, sensible, reliable human attendance is necessary twice daily, to check on accidents and illness if nothing else. If the owner is not free to attend, arrangements must be made with some other suitable person to take turns.

Back to Nature – with reservations

So often we hear people talking about horses at grass as being 'in natural conditions' and of horses who have been sick, injured or just in need of a break, being turned out for a 'nature cure'. True, a horse at grass is out in the open air, eating grass and wandering about more or less as he wishes, as he would be in nature, but that is where the similarity ends between nature and mere outdoor domesticity.

The fact that a horse is, by evolution, a creature of the plains and wide open spaces often leads people to think that, as he survived in the open in his wild state without human attention, so he can survive in an open field in domesticity. But this is not so, and for several reasons. Life in a truly natural, wild state is very different from life in a confined space, even if this confined space consists of several acres. One would need many acres of reasonable quality, sheltered and watered pastures before one could begin to emulate nature.

To appreciate the difference, consider what the terms 'nature' and 'natural conditions' mean. Perhaps the simplest and most direct definition is that the horse is living in conditions created by nature and to which nature adapted him by evolution. These conditions comprise hundreds of square miles of land with ground of varying texture and consistency, which wears down the horse's constantly growing hooves, and with water holes, lakes, streams and rivers to drink from, and a great variety of vegetation to provide the wide range of nutrients needed for robust health. There is also shelter in the form of caves, cliffs, rocks, thick clumps of trees or bushes, sheltered valleys, hills or just hollows in the ground, which feral and wild horses use to protect themselves from bitterly cold or wet, windy weather, and from the sun and flies.

The 'natural conditions' which most owners are able to provide do not nearly match up to the real ones. Turned out on relatively soft agricultural-type land, the horse's hooves soon become overgrown causing him inconvenience, even pain, and adversely affecting his ability to move about and exercise himself, so man-applied foot-trimming is needed. The grasses in the field may be too rich, restricted in range or unpalatable, or the land may be overstocked and become what is known as 'horse sick', where all the best grasses are over-grazed until they virtually cease to exist, leaving inedible herbage like docks, rank grass, growing nettles (horses relish them when cut and dead) and other weeds, not to mention poisonous plants, which all take over the land.

The water supply we believe to be adequate may, in reality, be insufficient, dirty or stagnant and polluted. And the shelter facilities in most horses' fields are practically non-existent. Wind and rain pass straight through man-made fences and thin, straggly hedges, and there may be no over-head shelter at all.

Overcrowding, which rarely occurs in the wild, results in a build-up on the pasture of the microscopic larvae of internal parasites, which the horses ingest with the grass. In nature, many different species of animal commonly graze together. This not only means that each kind picks out its own favourite grasses (what one leaves another will eat) but the different species eat with the grass the larvae of the other species' parasites, which usually die in an unnatural host.

There are advantages to both ways of life, wild/feral and domesticated. Domesticated horses are normally protected by their owners from carnivorous hunting animals which may exist in their part of the world. The horse is not denied leadership as he has a substitute for the stallion (or, more likely, the matriarchal mare) in a human who makes major decisions and should provide all the horse needs in the way of food, water, shelter and general care. However, the horse does usually have to work, sometimes quite hard. He cannot please himself when he comes and goes but has to wait for his master or mistress to take or let him out or to provide fresh pasture. He also has to put up with various fussings which he may dislike, and is completely dependent on humans for all he needs to keep him well and happy.

The big advantage of being wild is the horse's freedom to do as he likes within the constrictions of his herd's social rules. He has many square miles of country to call home, which amply satisfy his natural, evolved instinct to roam. He is not restricted to bare, unpalatable pastures when he has been in one place too long (unless in competition with domesticated animals like cattle and sheep turned on to his range) but can move on to fresh grazing. He is also not obliged to huddle miserably behind a thin, holey hedge vainly seeking shelter on a cold, wet night, but can roam on to a more sheltered area to rest.

But this wonderful freedom so beloved of all creatures, including Man, has to be paid for. The wild horse in many parts of the world means 'food' to carnivorous animals, and a wild or feral horse has no one to care for him or lessen his suffering when ill or hurt; he must fend for himself. His alternative is death, from disease, starvation, thirst or predation.

The object of domesticating an animal is to use him to make life easier or more enjoyable for ourselves. As we are going to ask more of him in domestication in terms of physical output than would be asked in nature, we must improve his lot to ensure he acquires and maintains the increased state of health and fitness needed for him to work or breed to our satisfaction. If the 'natural' conditions we offer in domesticity are not good enough, we must make up for them artificially. In any case, those of us who care about our horses will want to make life comfortable and happy for them, and not want to see them eking out a mere existence in inadequate conditions.

It is not clever to make animals rough it by subjecting them to harsh lifestyles. This sort of treatment does not harden them up but results in misery and physical deterioration, even in death. Harsh conditions are particularly dangerous for old animals, which have lost the resistance and strength of their youth, yet are the category of animal most often subjected to neglect of this sort, and for youngsters, both before and after birth, resulting in stunted growth and development and impaired constitution for the rest of that creature's probably shortened life.

2 Handling

Apart from knowledge of how to feed and generally care for a horse, of his basic physiology and of the horse as an individual, there is another important aspect of management which can make or mar the relationship between horse and owner, and that is handling. Horse handling and management is very much a 'contact' activity and the handling part, in particular, is one which is often learned the hard way. Just as there is an old saying 'You're not a horseman until you've fallen off' (and very often not then either) you might also say you don't know how to handle horses until you have been kicked, bitten, trodden on, pinned in a corner by a pair of threatening hooves or just a black look, or chased out of a field by a horse you were trying to catch. Even if these experiences do not teach you the right way to do things, they at least teach you the wrong way – plus how strong, heavy and formidable horses are if you get on the wrong side of them. Most of the time, successful horse handling amounts to knowing the correct way to do something, knowing the individual horse's quirks and having the mental presence to put mind over matter and act with calmness and confidence.

Because horses evolved as prey animals they developed an alert, nervous nature, always on the lookout for predators and ready to fly off the instant danger threatened. This behaviour and instinct is still very strong in domesticated horses, simmering just beneath the surface of their acquired *savoir-faire*; even the best trained and worldly-wise horse can be startled by an unaccustomed sight or sound, a thoughtless movement at the wrong time or even a figment of his imagination.

Turning a horse out

Unless a horse associates his field with unpleasantness, he

will be eager to get back to it and keen to greet his friends over the gate. They, in turn, may be milling around generally making life a bit difficult for you. It is tempting to half open the gate and bundle your horse through, somehow slipping off his headcollar in the process, to avoid entering the field and possibly getting hassled by its occupants; but a half-open gate can leave little room for your horse to pass through and he might knock himself on it or the gatepost.

The safe way to lead a horse through a gate is to hold the horse in the hand nearest the gatepost and open the gate with your free hand, allowing enough room for you and the horse to pass through without injury and *keeping hold of the gate all the time*. As the horse executes a perfect turn on the forehand round to face the gate, you begin closing the gate at once with your free hand and fasten it securely again. You and your horse are now facing the gate and you have performed a neat, nifty movement giving you both safe access to the field without allowing other horses to escape. Now lead the horse a few paces into the field and turn him round again to face the gate, release him and step back. If he whirls round on his hind legs and gallops off with a buck and a kick, you will now be well out of the way of his heels. If you release him while he is still facing into the field he might accidentally knock you down or kick you in passing in his haste to get to the middle of the field. (He is unlikely to want to gallop off towards the gate he has just come through!)

Taking him out through the gate is similarly easily achieved once the horse gets the hang of the sequence of movements involved. Again, hold the horse in the hand nearest the gatepost and open the gate with your other, free hand wide enough for you both to pass through safely; another turn on the forehand from the horse while you pull the gate closed behind you and fasten it, having kept hold of the gate all the time, as before, to prevent it swinging or being pushed open further by other horses, and you have safely extricated yourself and your horse without letting others get out.

A well hung gate which will open and close easily with one hand is a big help, as is a catching pen (detailed in Chapter 3).

Catching

Catching horses can be a process fraught with frustration, anger, blood, sweat and tears as there is nothing more infuriating than a horse that will not be caught. One learns quite early on that it is pointless running after a horse, who can keep well out of a human's way by simply trotting, never mind proceeding at a Derby winner's speed, so again it is mind over matter.

It is always said you should approach a horse from the shoulder, but the reason has never satisfactorily been explained to me. Whichever direction you use, except directly behind, he will see you and take evasive action if he wants. If you do approach from behind and he does not spot you until you are nearly upon him, you run the risk of being inadvertently or purposely kicked.

To catch a horse who is co-operative, you simply walk calmly and confidently up to him, slip on a headcollar (or bridle if you are going to lead him on a road where more control is needed), and you've got him. Horses who are slightly difficult to catch are often quite amenable if you can get them to come to you for something desirable, like oats or sugar lumps. A friend of mine had a horse who was impossible to catch if she went after him, so she would sit in the field eating sweets out of a very rustly, large white bag. The horse eventually gave in to curiosity and temptation, approached for his share and she would catch hold of the short rope hanging from his headcollar. He was not allowed a sweet until he had permitted her to grasp the rope, and would then come quietly.

I have spent many hair-raising hours trying to help other people catch their horses by various means, such as herding them into a corner, sometimes with a long rope, buckets of food and a positive army of helpers, and occasionally have succeeded, but who wants to go through that performance every time the horse is needed? A much better way is to try to effect a permanent cure and I have found the following very effective.

Buy yourself a brightly coloured bucket for water, something distinctive from an ordinary feed bucket, and give the horse regular drinks from it or at least show him it full of water, so he gets to know it contains water. Then turn him out in a field with no water supply or block off the existing one somehow. Turn out with him a horse who is easy to catch.

Go to the field and take the full water bucket to offer to the horse. If he approaches, make sure you do not let him drink until he has let you catch hold of the short rope hanging from his headcollar (I am presuming he is so equipped if he is difficult to catch). If he refuses to let you catch him, take the water out of the field without letting him drink. The 'good' horse should be allowed to drink its fill, so you will probably need a helper with an identical bucket.

Return a few hours later, let the good horse drink again, but do the same with the bad one – no catch, no drink. Repeat this procedure every few hours until the horse *will* let you catch him. If the horse has gone half a day or more without drinking, limit him to half a bucketful on the first and second occasions and thereafter let him have a full bucketful. I have used this method on two particularly bad-to-catch animals. The first was permanently cured, the second relapsed after a few weeks and was put through the treatment again. The last I heard of him he had remained good to catch.

Once the horse seems cured, return him to his original field or restore his water supply, when he will almost certainly remain good, having established the habit within himself of allowing you to catch him, although you may always need food of some kind as an attraction. Do, however, always remember to insist on being able to catch hold of him *before* he gets his reward.

The above method works better in mid-summer to autumn, when the grass is drier and the weather warm. It works even better in large, grassless yards or dirt corrals, although these are rare in Britain, as the horse can get no water from the grass. I would not use the method, however, in circumstances where horses are receiving only hay and concentrates, which are comparatively dry foods, as digestive troubles could occur through lack of moisture. The treatment does not work so well using food instead of water, particularly when the grass is good.

There will always be the animal who remains almost impossible to catch all its life and I feel such horses, who relapse no matter what cure you try, can only be abandoned to an indoor life.

If you are unfortunate enough to have to turn out your horse with another which is bad tempered with humans, life can become fraught with anxiety and foreboding every time you have to go to the field (which will be at least twice a day). Provided the animal is not actually dangerous (in which case it should be removed from the field for the sake of all concerned) attack is often the best form of defence. Such horses are often bullies and if they come at you with teeth bared, ears back and an unmistakable 'get-out-of-my-field' look, try going towards them smartly, making yourself look aggressive, waving arms, headcollar or a big stick, and bellowing at them. A smart rap on the advancing nose with said big stick has worked well for me several times in the past, and I was never harassed by those particular animals (often ponies) again. A horse which subsequently turns on you with determined-looking heels should, in my view, be swiftly removed from the field as walloping it on the rump will not usually work. Disturbing the peace warrants solitary confinement.

A lot depends on your personality. If you appear strong, confident and knowledgeable to a bully horse, it will often back down, but if it thinks you are weak it will take advantage. A bit of acting ability on your part can be a big help!

Tying up

If you have to care for your horse entirely in the field, having no stable, you will need a secure tying-up point, preferably a proper ring bolted through the wall of the shed, if it is strong enough, or to one of the support posts. Here you will be under cover and, if you temporarily block off the entrance to the shelter with sliprails, you can tend to your horse in peace.

Leave the sliprails on the ground outside close up to the wall of the shelter where they are less likely to be trodden on by the horses.

If, for some reason, you cannot tie up your horse in the shelter, try to find a convenient tree branch or, if all else fails, use one of the fence *support* posts, never one of the rails which will probably break quite easily if the horse takes a determined pull backwards. A horse can exert a pull of roughly one and a half times his own weight, so you can see that whatever you intend to tie him to must be virtually an immovable object. Of course, his leadrope and headcollar would probably break first if he were exerting a really determined pull on a strong anchoring point, and many people maintain that horses should be tied up to a loop of string so that they will break free rather than risk breaking the structure or their headcollars, or risk injuring themselves.

My own feeling is that horses should be taught when young to tie up – and to learn that they cannot break free – not by force but by means of a long rope to their headcollar dee, through a ring on the wall and back to their handler's hand. Then, by give and take, the handler can give some rope when the youngster pulls back, and gently bring him back again. The horse does not then get the feeling of restriction imposed by the 'old school' who maintain they should be left securely tied up and left to 'fight it out with themselves'. The method may well work, but I feel the horse's spirit and personality lose something in the process.

With a mature horse who has learned that he can break free (a truly accursed vice), improvement can be effected by a friend standing behind and to one side of the horse with a stiff-bristled yard broom while you groom him. Then, when the horse makes to pull back, a couple of sharp scrubs under the tail will warn him to think better of it. Another method is to fasten a lungeing rein to the headcollar D, back under the horse's tail and through the dee again to the tie-ring (it can be secured from dropping down by a driving pad or by running it through run-up stirrups on a saddle). Then when the horse pulls back he will feel the rein behind his thighs and few horses will resist against that.

Whatever method is used, it is essential that a horse which has to be tended outdoors must be able to be tied up reliably and safely. Always use a conventional slip knot which you can pull undone with one jerk (a half bow) in case of emergency.

Friends and enemies

Horses are gregarious animals craving the company of their own kind. Although this may be inconvenient to us at times, it is understandable, as they evolved as herd animals always surrounded by at least a few others of their species. For millions of years they lived in this way and for good reason – there is safety, in the wild, in numbers. A solitary animal is easy prey to a carnivore in search of a meal, but if there is a herd of you, there is a good chance it will pick someone else!

This, and many other aspects of behaviour, has become instinctive in the horse, and instinctive behaviour is not wiped out by a mere few thousand years of breeding in domestication. The need for the company of others, even if only one, of its own kind is firmly ingrained in most horses. There are a few animals who do not seem to care for other equine company but they are rare.

Most horses, then, should be provided with company to ensure their happiness and contentment, and although animals such as goats and donkeys are often used as substitutes, there is really nothing quite like another horse, or a pony, as a companion. Anything else must seem rather like giving a human a chimpanzee to talk to.

Horses, like all animals, have their own code of social etiquette, and it is quite easy for an observer to discern which are the Boss Horses in given situations and which the underlings. The usual bones of contention among a herd of horses in a field are choice patches of grazing, water, shelter, chosen companions and, believe it or not, humans. When the human brings with it hay and other foods, there is another bone to fight over.

Sometimes there is an overall herd leader. In the wild this is usually an old, experienced, assertive mare rather than the stallion. She even bosses him about and tells him when he can mate her (as, indeed, do the other mares). In domesticated conditions, sometimes a mare and sometimes a gelding is boss. In many herds, however, you will find one particular animal has first choice where, say, food is concerned, another where access to the water trough is concerned, and so on. If an underling is sheltering under a particular tree and the Shelter Boss saunters over, all the latter may need to do to get the other horse to move is simply put its ears back, and sometimes not even that, so secure is its position. If a horse not so high up the Shelter Hierarchy comes along, however, it may need to do a bit more, not only ears back but maybe a quick nip or even a good bite, too. When two horses of similar rank have it out over a jointly desired property, the results can be serious indeed, particularly if the horses are shod. Severe kicking (resulting in, at worst, fractured bones) and biting take place, with ears back, tails thrashing and generally threatening looks.

It may be of some reassurance to know, however, that in a herd with an established membership and hierarchy, each animal knows its place and true fights are very rare. If two animals really form a seemingly permanent antagonistic relationship, their human owners must simply resolve never to turn them out within reach of each other, otherwise constant injuries will be the result.

Apart from physical injuries, a horse which is always being bullied by one or more others will be unhappy and under considerable stress. Stress seems to be a much-used word these days, and with good reason, for it is now known and accepted that mental stress, or rather too much of it, does lead to physical disorders of various sorts. A miserable horse will never thrive physically to its full potential and will be unable, therefore, to work as well for its owner as it would if happy and prospering. In any case, most owners will want their horses to be happy and so will do their best to create happy surroundings and lives for them.

Introducing a new horse
One situation, in connection with herd relationships, which

can cause a good deal of trouble is when one tries to introduce a new horse into an established herd. This will
inevitably completely upset the apple cart until the horses
sort out for themselves (and only they can do it) where the
newcomer is going to fit in. Even so, there is a good deal
humans can do to try to smooth out the wrinkles and avoid
as far as possible the serious fights which could ensue if the
introductions are wrongly carried out.

The worst way to introduce a new horse into a herd is
simply to open the field gate and bundle him through into
the mêlée of curious bodies on the other side, and just leave
them to get on with it. This method will almost certainly
result in a badly hurt newcomer and permanently soured
relationships between him and the others.

The correct way is to allow the new horse to make friends
with at least one of the herd first, preferably one fairly low
down in the general hierarchy (who might be glad of a new
friend) or one noted for its congenial attitude towards other
horses. These two should be led around in hand (wearing
bridles for extra control) and perhaps taken for a ride
together. If stables are available, they could perhaps be
stabled next to each other for a night, or just an hour or two,
and finally turned out together in a preferably small paddock
(where they cannot get up too much speed but can get out of
each other's way, if necessary), ideally with plenty of grass, to
take their minds off each other. There will be some nose and
tail smelling, a few squeals and a bit of stamping and
prancing around but, if care has been taken to match them
temperamentally and status-wise, there is almost certain to
be no real trouble.

The next stage should be to put these two *alone* into the
main field which is to be their home and gradually bring back
the other herd members, low-ranking ones first, one by one,
letting each new arrival have up to half an hour to fully assess
the newcomer, until the herd is complete. Again, there will
be some introductory sparring and maybe a couple of 'try-
outs', but there should be no serious problems.

This might all sound like too much of a palaver, but it is an
ideal way, and may not be possible in all circumstances.

Another method would be to put the newcomer *and his friend,* to prevent the sole horse trying to jump in to the others, into a safely fenced adjoining field so that the rest of the herd can weigh them up over the fence. It is better for the horses not to be able to touch each other over the fence if at all possible, but this may be difficult to arrange. After half a day in this situation, preferably more, the two chums can usually be put in with the others with little trouble, although two people should stay around for up to half an hour in case of trouble should the horses need separating again.

The new horse will settle in surprisingly quickly, if properly introduced into the herd and, likewise, the others will accept him. On the other hand, if the introduction is carried out wrongly, the animals could well be permanent enemies and the newcomer constantly unhappy – a pointless and miserable situation for all concerned.

Numbers
The personalities and temperaments of the horses turned out together will ultimately decide the success of their relationships. Numbers do not normally matter and, in any case, horses will be coming and going into and out of the field as their owners arrive to work them or return them after exercise, so, especially in communally used fields, it will be impossible to always have a set number of animals turned out together.

It follows that there will be times when an animal may well be left alone for a certain period of time, which it will probably not like. If it cannot be safely shut in at such times, the only way to teach it to put up with such a situation is to leave it to get used to the idea. It is true that animals which object to this can work themselves up into a sweat and start charging the fences and gates trying to get out, so the fencing will have to be truly deterring, high and strong. Only experience will tell whether such an animal is going to learn to tolerate occasional solitude, and most do; if it does not, its owner will simply have to accept that it can only be turned out if there is at least one other animal in the field.

If only two horses are turned out together as a regular

procedure, another problem arises in that they can become impossibly attached to each other. Not only does the one left behind behave as described above, but the one taken out for work will be an absolute pest, whinnying to its soul-mate, not working well and, in bad cases, jibbing and napping and becoming not merely a nuisance (and therefore not enjoyable) to own but dangerous as well.

A horse *must*, almost above all else, learn to go where and how its rider or driver tells it, alone or in company, and this takes very firm, determined and knowledgeable handling – and you must win the 'fight' as soon as trouble starts to develop. If you are at all unsure of your capabilities to do this, I strongly urge you to engage professional help, otherwise you may well find that you end up not being able to use your horse at all.

3 Accommodation and Facilities

To a horse kept at grass, obviously his whole world is his field. He will probably spend at least twenty-two hours out of twenty-four in it, and it needs to be a place which offers him health, happiness, comfort, safety and, as far as is possible in an open field, security.

Much depends on what the horse's owner expects of the field. Does he or she want it to provide most of the horse's food, or is it to be merely somewhere to put the horse because there is no stable?

This book is mainly for people who are keeping horses at grass twenty-four hours a day at any particular time of year. Therefore, even if they are happy to provide their horse's food in the form of concentrates and hay, for their horse's sake and their own convenience and peace of mind, they will need to consider the general suitability of the field.

Many owners know little about land and grass, and it is easy to think that any plot with practically anything growing on it will make a good enough home for a horse. But this is by no means the case. Most owners do not have their own land and are not in a position to be too choosy, but the fact remains that an unsuitable environment can make life difficult and worrying for the owner and most unpleasant, even dangerous, for the horse.

Type of field

The best horse paddocks are on light, well drained land which does not easily waterlog in wet weather or bake hard in dry. (The quality or 'richness' – or otherwise – of the land and, hence, its productive abilities, can be to some extent changed by treatments and fertilisers, about which more in Chapter 4.) Fine grained soils like clay quickly go from one extreme to the other while peaty soils are only really good in the driest weather, soon becoming sticky or flooded at other times. Sandy soils can be good and are often naturally well drained, although they will not grow the lushest grass. For horses, however, this is not important, as protein-rich herbage causes digestive troubles in them. The ideal soil is what every farmer wants, a rich brown loam. The rock over which the soil lies can determine soil quality, eg limestone areas are traditionally desirable for breeding bloodstock because of the calcium (for bone and teeth development) they impart to the soil. But nutrients can be added to the diet easily enough in deficient areas.

Drainage
Drainage is vital especially for a field which is to be used heavily in wet seasons. A couple of horses living on a wet and, particularly, a small field will soon poach it into a morass of liquid mud quite unfit for habitation.

Wet land is cold land. Not only does it make the growth of ample good grass difficult by starving the roots of air and warmth, it creates favourable conditions for mud fever. If the land is your own or you have it on lease for some years, it could be worth putting in a drainage system to make it usable, healthy and productive, otherwise you will be able to use it only in dry seasons. If the land is also used for agricultural purposes (say, fattening bullocks, which is excellent for horse pastures incidentally) you could also get a grant towards the work.

Even in dry weather, it is often possible to tell if a field is too wet by the type of herbage growing on it. If there are rushes or marsh grasses with round, spiky blades, forget it. You will need a reclamation programme rather than a drainage system to make it acceptable.

Fields with natural drainage in the form of a gentle slope to some outlet such as a ditch, stream or road with drains are good, as are those drained by the old method of ridge and furrow, where the land has wide, gently domed ridges, the water running away in the furrows. Fields of both these types are good for horses as they help keep them muscled and balanced in their paces. Flat fields do not have this advantage and often need expensive drainage systems installed as the water has no route of running away. They become water-logged, even flooded, very easily, particularly in lowland areas. Such fields need deep ditches on all sides cleared out regularly, to take the water, and even then may not be a success. They also tend to seethe with flies in summer.

Other considerations
Steep hillside fields, too, have disadvantages. Apart from the fact that it can be impossible to get machinery on them for agricultural jobs, they can be uncomfortable and wearing for the horses, who are constantly bracing themselves against the gradient and can neither lie nor stand in comfort. There must be at least one flat, sheltered area where they can relax without having to combat the slope. Such fields are unsafe for in-foal mares, and youngsters who gallop about a lot, as they cause falls and stumbles which can bring about abortions and other injuries.

Although unpleasant, hard ground is less of a problem than mud as the horses can at least be put on it. Jarred limbs from excessive galloping occur most often when horses are overfed, underworked or forced to charge away from flies through lack of shelter.

Another point to consider is whether the field is sheltered or exposed. A fairly sheltered field is best even if your horse is quite commonly bred. He will then not be battling against the full brunt of the weather and will not need so much food to keep flesh on him in winter. Some people argue that an exposed field is best in summer as the constant breeze keeps flies away, but in my experience the difference is minute.

New leys (fields which have been seeded less than a year) are not really suitable for horses. Unless the seed mix contained herbs and a wide variety of grasses, the herbage will most likely be too limited. This is usually the case with mixtures sown for cattle. It is not until the second year that indigenous herbs and weeds appear, providing interest and variety (of taste and nutrition) for the horses, plus essential nutrients often lacking in cultivated grasses. Also, in young fields the turf has been destroyed by ploughing. After years, sometimes centuries, of undisturbed growth, the roots of grasses and other plants form an underground network, a 'cushion', which makes the perfect surface for horses' legs and hooves. Old turf is heavenly to walk on. It feels springy underfoot and absorbs the jar when the foot hits the ground. It is also more resistant to the destructive action of hooves. With new leys, the ground is still loose, there is no protective network of roots and the grass is easily pushed in or torn out and wasted.

Orchards and woods

These do not make good homes for horses. The grass under trees, although it may look luscious, is often poor and sour as it lacks sunlight and is not cared for like genuine pasture. It often contains much useless stuff like old matted grass, moss or rotten fruit, not to mention poisonous plants, conkers and acorns. Chemical residues from preparations sprayed on fruit trees may linger and poison the horses, who also often make themselves ill by eating windfalls or pulling fruit off trees. The ground in woods and spinneys is often very rough, and I once saw a pony with the most sickening injury to his leg, caused by an old, forgotten trap hidden by grass and brambles.

Generally, I should prefer to fence off such areas even though they might seem to offer good shelter, unless one can be quite sure none of the above dangers exist.

Size of field

Generally speaking, if the land is in good condition and producing varied, medium quality grass ideal for horses, 2 acres (.8ha) properly managed should just support one horse in light work all year round (plus supplementary feeding in winter) or two horses during spring and summer. As a horse should always have a companion, this means that for two horses getting much of their food from the grass, at least 4 acres (1.6ha) will be needed on a year-round basis. The poorer the land or grass, the more you will need. In fact, horses keep happier and healthier with a large area of medium to poor grazing than a small one of rich grass; they have more space to roam and have to walk and exercise more in search of their food.

As will be shown in the next chapter, the land must be divided if it is to be well-managed and productive. It is best to try and keep one's driest land mainly for winter use, resting it as much as possible during summer, and laying off the wetter land in winter. If renting land, try to acquire one field for spring and summer, changing for a drier and more sheltered one in winter.

Hedges and trees

These are a definite advantage to a paddock. Apart from providing interesting titbits, as horses often nibble them, they give some protection from the weather. One of the best windbreaks possible is a belt of trees and/or a high, thick hedge on the windward side of a field. The horses will gather there during wind and rain and be grateful for the protection. Trees, if thick enough, also give overhead shelter and hedges, if well kept, make excellent fencing.

To be effective as either windbreaks or fencing, hedges must be periodically trimmed, although left high and thick and, ideally, laid. A farm worker or agricultural contractor can do this and the finished job has an aesthetic as well as a practical value. If a hedge is left to grow wild it becomes thin and straggly with large gaps which not only invite horses to escape but allow wind and rain right through. Laying (which involves reinforcing the hedge with its own branches laid diagonally across it) strengthens the hedge and helps fill in gaps. A well done job, although expensive because it is a skilled craft, should last many years. A hedge can be left at 5ft (1.5m) or higher, and left fairly thick by the trimmer, when it will appear neat, discourage the horses from jumping out and provide an effective windbreak.

Man-made fencing

Fencing can be an expensive item, particularly if much new

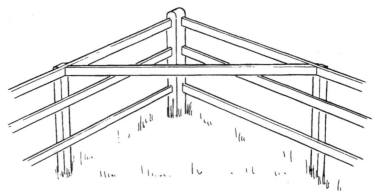

Sharply angled corners can be dangerous to galloping horses, and to timid animals who can be cornered and bullied. This bar, fixed at a safe height, will steer a fast-moving horse round the corner, and will prevent one horse being hemmed in by others

material is needed, but few things detract more from the appearance and safety of a field than dilapidated, unsuitable or badly erected fences.

Effective fencing can save a great deal of inconvenience and expense to the owner, whose liability it is if his horses stray from their proper place. Any damage they cause to neighbouring property, not to mention road accidents, is the responsibility of their owner. In addition is the pain and suffering caused to humans involved in an accident, and to the horses themselves if they are injured or eat a surfeit of growing corn in the next field. So apart from an insurance policy with a trustworthy company to guard against damages, the provision of effective fencing really is a must. Some insurance companies may not pay out in a claim action if a horse has been enabled to stray through neglect of the owner to provide proper fencing.

If your land lacks suitable natural hedges, even those reinforced by man-made fencing in the gaps, you will have to provide an alternative. No fencing should be lower than the height of the horse's back, with the lowest strand or rail no lower than 12 in (30cm) from the ground to reduce the likelihood of a horse getting a leg over it and damaging both himself and the fence trying to pull it back.

Rounding off the corners of the field helps prevent

galloping horses colliding with the corner by steering them round it. This can be done by erecting the fencing in curves rather than corners or, with existing fencing, by fixing a 6ft (1.8m) rail diagonally across the corner at horse's shoulder height.

Wooden support posts should be sunk into the ground for one-third of their length so that when the horses rub against them they will not become easily loosened. Needless to say, wooden structures should be treated with a reliable wood preserver, especially if going underground. Many suppliers now have their own excellent systems of preservation for their products and creosote is now largely being superseded.

Wooden posts and rails (preferably hardwood for wear) are still considered the most traditional and safest fencing by many horsemen, and are still the most expensive. Some economy can be made, though, by buying only two-rail fencing which is quite adequate for mature horses. The bottom rail, in this case, can be about 2ft (60cm) from the ground. Breeding stock and ponies should have four- or three-rail fencing respectively to prevent foals and small ponies getting through the gaps. With foals, there is a danger they will roll or lie down near the fence and, in getting up, end up on the other side of it with panic stations resulting, so the bottom rail for them should be low enough to prevent them doing this, about a foot (30cm) high.

The tops of the posts should be flush with the top rail, never above it, to minimise the dreadful injuries which the protrusions can inflict on horses trying to jump out, and to prevent their catching in a loose headcollar. The rails themselves should be fixed on the inside of the posts, making a smooth barrier for a horse rubbing along them. Horses can injure themselves on fence posts inside the rails. If it is impossible to arrange the rails correctly, or where a single fence separates two fields, run a single rail at horse's shoulder height on the offending side.

Plain wire fencing on wooden posts is a fair and cheaper alternative to wooden rails provided it is kept properly strained and taut. It does have the disadvantage of the whole of one strand collapsing all along its length in the case of

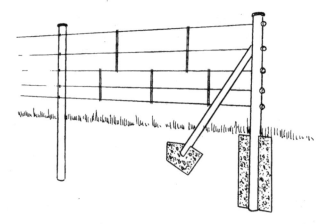

Plain wire dropper fencing (which can be electrified). The vertical dropper rods enable the posts to be spaced more widely apart (for economy) and will prevent full strands of wire collapsing if broken

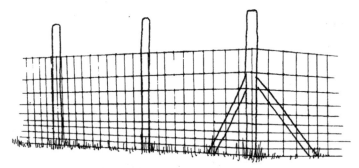

Resilient wire mesh fencing with the lower meshes sufficiently small to prevent a horse's hoof passing through; suitable where horses are grazed with sheep. The joints between strands should be securely fixed to prevent movement. If galloping horses collide with this type of fencing, it tends to 'bounce' them off unhurt

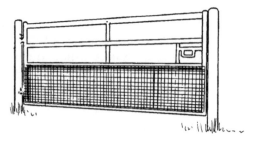

A strong, safe, tubular metal gate, the bottom part filled in with strong mesh to prevent horses' legs getting caught through the bars. The catch is safe and unobtrusive, and easily padlocked to the gatepost with a chain

damage, instead of just one section breaking, but this is avoided with *dropper fencing* which has strainer rods vertically supported on the wires between posts, so restricting sagging to just that one area. Because the strainers support the wire and help keep it taut, the posts can be fewer and further between than with other types of fence, so it is economical.

Resilient fencing in the form of *wire mesh*, heavy gauge, is becoming more popular, particularly on establishments catering for more than one type of grazing animal. The type recommended for horses has lower meshes small enough to prevent a horse's hoof passing through them. With conventional sheep fencing, horses frequently get their legs through the squares with disastrous results.

There is always a possibility, with most wire fencing, of the wire mysteriously finding its way between the horse's hoof and his shoe in accidents or skirmishes near the fence, when the shoe might be ripped off as the horse struggles to free himself, causing a badly torn foot.

Resilient fencing works on the principle that horses colliding with the fence (a quite common occurrence) are bounced off it harmlessly instead of breaking through it or hurting themselves on a rigid structure such as a stone wall or iron railings. Post and rail fencing is often purposely designed with rails weak enough to break if the horse hits them hard enough (rather than the horse breaking his leg) but then you have the problem of an inviting gap being left in the fence.

Flexible fencing has the advantages of being resilient and easily seen by the horses, being usually white, while being in rail, rather than wire, form. It consists of flexible synthetic material which comes usually in a roll and which is simply nailed to conventional support posts. It is excellent for improving existing fencing, instead of wire, and it has been found that often a single 'rail' fixed round the top of a fence is sufficient to warn the horses of its presence and cause them to respect the fence. It is also rotproof and chew resistant, unlike wooden fencing. For those who have to move fields often, it can be a boon as it can simply be removed, rolled up, and reinstated in a new field much more easily than other materials.

Another form of take-away fencing which, I feel, is not made sufficient use of for horses is *electric fencing*. Provided horses are taught properly about it this can be a really effective way of keeping them away from taboo areas such as dangerous dykes, ponds, bogs and faulty fencing. Various makes and systems are advertised in equestrian journals, both mains and battery operated (the latter being especially useful for rented grazing). Not only can it be used to divide a field and so help with correct pasture management, it can easily be removed when you leave and can be used to transform a paddock with unsafe fencing into an acceptable home for your horse. The newest type is in the form of an easily-seen twinkling electrified metal tape.

Electric fencing can be used as the top strand of a wire fence, can be run inside the posts of a conventional wooden fence to keep horses away from it, or used alone on its own insulated rods. Although many people would regard the latter arrangement as temporary, it is a fact that some horses live for long periods surrounded by this type of electric fencing and, because they have a healthy respect for it, will not even go near it, let alone try to jump it.

To introduce a horse to electric fencing, moisten his nose (for added 'impact') and lead him up to the fence, pressing his nose gently but firmly against it. He will receive a sufficient shock to make him jump back, so be ready for him, but will not be hurt. Take him further along the fence and do the same. On the second occasion he will usually decline your invitation. Make sure you lead him all round the field wherever the fencing is and show it to him.

Barriers to avoid include stone walls (very good for breaking horses' legs), wire gardening mesh and chestnut palings (too weak), iron railings with sharp metal joints and spikes (death traps) and the all-too-commonly-seen barbed wire.

Unfortunately, most horse owners enquiring about rented grazing will be confronted with barbed wire, and although it is true that horses can graze happily for years surrounded by this murderous stuff without coming to any harm, to me the situation likens itself to the Sword of Damocles. One day the sword will fall and your horse will come into contact with the fence. You could be lucky and have him escape with a few minor scratches. On the other hand, he could be scarred for life, or even rip his legs and/or body so badly that he is permanently crippled, which, in our economy, usually means he has to be destroyed.

What better case could there be for investing in your own set of electric fencing? Of course, it will cost money, but could mean the difference between accepting an otherwise suitable field (and they are hard enough to find as it is) or continuing your anxious search further afield – or between a safe horse and a fatally injured one. It is worth considering.

Gates

Horses often congregate round the gateway, perhaps at feeding time, when they want to he brought in or are lonely, so it is obvious that gates must be strong and safe. Whether of wood or metal, they should be hung so that their top rail is, again, at horse's back height or slightly higher. If this means adding another rail on the bottom for foals, so be it. The top rails can be horizontal, but if the lower ones also are they should be filled in from the inside with strong metal mesh. Some horse requisite suppliers stock good tubular metal gates with the lower halves of vertical tubing, which are filled in with mesh to prevent legs getting through in impatience or excitement.

It helps to have a gate hung so it swings closed when you let go, rather than open! A gate which has to be lifted bodily (often with two already full hands) before it can be moved is not only annoying when one is trying to manoeuvre horses in or out of the field, but dangerous when the horses are milling around trying to get into your buckets of food. You need as few hindrances as possible so it pays to get the gate properly hung.

It can be a tricky operation, trying to get one horse into or out of a field with several others in it, but the job can be

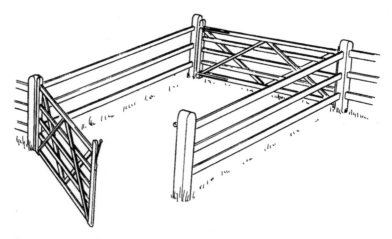

This catching pen enables horses to be taken through or brought out of a field without danger of other occupants escaping during the process

made much easier with a 'catching pen'. Here, the gate from the road, yard or wherever leads into a pen at least 12ft (3.65m) square, with another gate at the other end leading into the field. You open wide the outside gate, lead the horse in, turn yourselves round comfortably to close the gate and finally open the gate into the field and take him in. In this way, if the other horses wangle their way through the field gate, they will not be able to escape because you will have shut the gate leading to the road. Similarly, if your own horse breaks away from you he cannot go anywhere he shouldn't.

A safe width for a gate is about 5ft (1.5m) as this allows enough room for horse and handler to pass through in comfort. However, the width is less important (provided it is not ridiculously narrow) than the correct, calm way of passing through it, as described in Chapter 2.

Nuts and bolts used for securing hinges should be the smooth-headed type if on the inside, otherwise sharp edges should be filed off. The hinges should be the fixed type and not those with open tops which can be lifted off by the horse getting his neck under the top bar. If this type has been used the gate should be chained round the hinges to keep it on. There are several types of fastener for gates. Ordinary bolts and hunt catches (with a long vertical spring handle so that

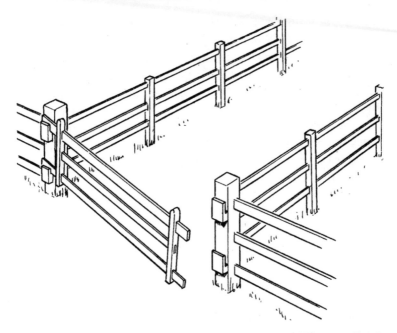

'Lanes' between fields enable normally incompatible neighbours to live in adjoining fields without being able to contact each other. On studs, this means that stock can be led freely around without passing through occupied paddocks. The slipgate is a refinement of the plain sliprail system. It is simple to construct, cheaper than a proper gate and light enough to be lifted with one hand when leading a horse. It is more secure than ordinary, separate sliprails and easier to operate

they can be opened from horseback) are soon fathomed out by horses, as are hook-type fasteners. A quick, secure way of fastening a gate is to have a length of wide-linked chain passing round the end of the gate and the post, being clipped together through its links with a strong spring clip, such as from the end of a worn-out headcollar rope. Stapling the chain to the gate and clipping the free end to a staple in the gatepost is good provided the staples are well in and firm. Tying the gate with rope or twine has often resulted in horses eventually undoing the knots or biting through the fabric.

Sliprails, slipgates and cattle grids
Cheaper than gates, *sliprails* should be strong, smooth poles (two or three depending on the height of the fence and the

size of the animals in the field) which slot into holders on each gatepost. Holders with open tops are useless unless the rails are fastened in at both ends, as horses soon learn to lift them out. A secure fastening is to have a heavy-duty nut and bolt (kept lightly oiled) passing through aligned holes drilled through the holder and pole. Even with enclosed holders, some horses can learn to jiggle the poles sideways, so it is always safer to secure one end of each pole. For safety's sake, the poles should be let down completely when the horse is passing through.

Slipgates are simply a framework looking like a gate, but slotting on to holders, as shown in the illustration. Again, their advantage over a gate is simply economy and, like sliprails, they are not so convenient for the handler, although effective in use.

Cattle grids are lethal to horses who are not usually in the least deterred by them. They wander unconcernedly across and fall with their legs trapped between the metal slats. I have seen more than one horse suffer the most horrible injuries this way, sometimes resulting in permanent hideous scars on the limbs. One pony I knew, having once been injured in a grid, was later returned to the field by his owner who thought he would have 'learned his lesson'. Certainly he did not walk across the grid again, but took to jumping it quite happily.

The need for shelter

Shelter seems to be the most neglected aspect of the management of horses at grass, even more neglected than feeding. The horse's natural coat and grease do not give anything like the protection often imagined. Nature intended these only as partial protection and without additional shelter horses suffer much more than people realise, or wish to admit.

A common remark seems to be: 'There's no point giving a horse a shelter, he wouldn't use it anyway.' This statement is often just an excuse for not having a shed, and unfounded, too, for I have only ever met three animals in my life who refused to enter a suitable shelter and in each case it was because it was frightened to do so.

(Reasons for this fear could be: (1) a bully horse inside the shed keeping out a more timid one; (2) the shed appearing dark so the horse cannot see that it is safe inside; (3) the entrance being badly poached, which will put off a sensitive individual; (4) the entrance being too low and/or narrow so that the horse might feel unable to enter without injury; and (5) the horse associating the shed with some unpleasant incident such as being cornered in it and kicked by another horse or knocking himself on the way in or out.)

In winter, leafless hedges and trees offer very little protection from driving sleet, relentless, biting winds and penetrating rain, but horses still vainly gather round them and the ground there becomes poached into a mass of oozing mud. I have seen common-bred horses and Thoroughbreds alike with rotted feet, painfully swollen legs and raw backs from constantly standing in mud, soaked to the skin and frozen. Miserable and shivering, they huddle together seeking moral support from one another to enable them to bear the unbearable.

Horses like dry, still, cold weather and often play and roll in fresh snow. It is when the snow turns to slush, when the sleet and rain pour down for days or when the frost freezes the mud round their legs and the wet on their backs that they suffer. Bitter winds in addition double the effects of the cold and wet, and many horses each year die inwardly (and, indeed, actually) from being forced to endure these atrocious conditions.

In summer, life without a shed can be no less agonising for different reasons. Undoubtedly, the worst part of summer is the flies and midges which mercilessly torment horses from dawn to dusk. Even at night some insects are active, but the worst times of day are from mid-morning to early evening. Flies happily follow horses into the shade of trees, but only a small hard core seem to go into a man-made shelter.

Some flies feed off the secretions from a horse's eyes, sheath and dock, others bite him to suck his blood – but all of them are capable of inflicting severe torment. Because we tend to overestimate the protective qualities of the horse's natural defence mechanisms, it is necessary to stress the chain of events which occurs during attacks by flies, something I have witnessed many times in horses inadequately protected (by their owners) from fly-strike. Some individuals, as always, are more susceptible than others, but they *all* suffer.

Nature has bestowed some defences on the horse, such as a mane, forelock and long neck and head which, combined, enable him to reach almost any part of his forehand, and also a tail which, when long enough, can deal with the quarters. There is also a large, flat sheet of muscle just under the skin on the sides and shoulders which twitches off insects effectively.

There is one big drawback to these built-in mechanisms. To keep the flies at bay the horse has to keep up a ceaseless campaign of head-shaking, muscle-twitching, leg-stamping and tail-swishing which soon wears him down. He can make himself sore, even raw, by biting himself or rubbing on any convenient object to relieve the itching and eventually, driven half out of his mind from the torment, he starts to run – the horse's natural defence against anything with which he cannot cope. Flies cannot keep up with a galloping horse, so he gallops, and gallops, and gallops, until he can go no more. He stops from exhaustion, probably in a heaving sweat which attracts the flies even more – and once again they attack to crawl upon and irritate the most sensitive parts of his body and particularly any raw areas caused by rubbing or other wounds.

In the end, all the horse can do is stand defeatedly nodding his head up and down like clockwork in a futile attempt to free himself from his tormentors, his eyes half closed from the soreness and swelling they cause. The galloping on hard ground does damage, too. His legs and feet can become jarred to the point of lameness and his lungs and heart overstressed from the constant overwork. The eyes can ulcerate eventually and wounds become infected, which simply compounds the problem as the flies greedily feed on the discharges produced.

A good residual insect repellant (dealt with in Chapter 5) is an excellent preventative of fly-strike, but to get away from flies completely an effective shelter shed really is essential.

A shed should be regarded as a basic necessity for any horse out for more than a few hours a day at any time of year other than late spring, and even then freak conditions can occur. Any horse will use one once he has become used to it and, protected not only from flies and winter weather but from heat and sun, too, his condition will noticeably improve. Horses come to regard their shelter as their anchor, their home base, a welcoming haven to which they can thankfully and confidently retreat when things get rough, knowing they will find peace, shelter, probably hay except when grass is plentiful, and a soft, dry bed on which to lie and rest.

Shelter sheds

I hesitate to give too many requirements for a shelter as almost anything is better than nothing, but there are certain standards to aim for and below which a shed will become dangerous and possibly discouraging to the horse.

This barn provides safe shelter for several horses at once; note the high, wide entrance, deep-litter flooring and hayracks around the walls. The animals can be kept in spacious indoor accommodation at night or in bad weather or, with the gate chained back against the outside wall, can come and go as they wish

A practical shed large enough for two horses can be purchased new or constructed from second-hand materials. This shed has an economical single-pitched roof at a safe height, a strong, secure hayrack and deep-litter bedding to encourage the horses to lie down and rest. The open front has no projecting beams or support posts

Ideally, a shed should give as much space per horse as a stable. For two horses who are friendly towards each other, a smaller structure could be adequate, but where several horses are out together and/or there is any squabbling more room is needed to allow the underdog to manoeuvre himself out of the way. Although it might sound impracticably lavish, if there are any real problems of hierarchy, two sheds should be provided so that there is a better chance of at least one of them always being available to a victim of bullying. I have seen it happen so many times that the more timid horses are constantly kept out of the only shelter available, with a consequent deterioration in their physical condition and happiness.

Prefabricated shelters are sold by many firms advertising in horse journals. Cheaper ones can be provided by buying a used building, say from a farm sale or smallholder selling up, or there might already be a building in your field which, with some modification, can be made suitable for horses. For several horses, a disused barn, or part of one, can give shelter for all, with a high lofty ceiling providing headroom and preventing any sense of being closed in, which puts off some horses from using a shed. Satisfactory sheds can also be constructed out of straw bales and supporting wooden framework with a rigid waterproof material such as wood covered by roofing felt, or even corrugated asbestos or poly- thene for the roof.

The main points about shelters are that (1) they should be sited on the highest, driest part of the field to prevent the inside becoming wet, (2) they should have their backs to the prevailing wind (or where there is none, to the north or east so that the entrance faces south, preferably, or west), (3) they should have high, wide entrances to encourage the horses in and allow room for manoeuvre when several are trying to get in at once, (4) they should not be set against a fence but have room all round to avoid crushing, and (5) they should be free of all projections, rusty nails, splintered wood and so on which could harm the horses; windows should be barred up and buildings with low rafters shunned.

Most shelters are rectangular and have the whole of one long side left out as an entrance. These work well, but provide no shelter from the front should the wind change direction. Do not, however, remove only one half of a long side leaving the other intact as this forms a 'cul-de-sac' inside where a horse can be cornered and injured. If the shed is big enough, have two 10ft (3m) wide entrances on each end of the front, otherwise it is safer to remove the whole side. A single pitch roof, sloping to the back of the shed obvi- ously, is quite adequate and should, at its lowest point, provide at least 2ft (60cm) headroom, preferably much more. Semi-circular shelters (rarely seen) are ideal, as there are no corners into which a victim can be hemmed. He can simply run round the wall and out.

Make the structure as strong as possible to withstand kicks and rubbing, and make provision for providing hay inside the shed, either by means of tie-rings bolted through for haynets or by fixing a cattle-type hayrack down the back wall with the top just above horse's head height. Keep the shelter well strawed down and the droppings picked up, and I am sure you will find your horses treat it as a real home and will show their gratitude in their condition.

Bedding

A concrete base is not necessary for a shelter as the horses do not often stale (urinate) inside. They do droppings, though, and these must be removed daily if you want to avoid an indoor muck-heap. Keep the bedding clean and as thick as for a stable. Used bedding can be scattered (minus droppings) on badly poached areas, such as the shelter entrance, gateways, round watering points and other areas where horses congregate, to help reduce this problem. These areas will not grow much grass anyway, so the practice will do nothing but good. Other substances which can be used to reduce poaching include sand, fine cinders and fine shale. Never, though, tip a load of rubble down as the stones and bricks can cut and bruise the hooves and lower legs. It also presents very rough, unreliable footing to the horses, who may become reluctant to step on it until forced by intense thirst or need of rest and shelter.

If, when you erect your shed, there is grass growing on the floor inside, remember your horses will eat it, until it withers and dies, and will take in any bedding on top. Therefore, use only straw bedding in the meantime as the inadvertent eating of other materials can cause colic.

In Chapter 4, on grassland management, the need for a rota in the use of fields is discussed. By using a little ingenuity, and ground conditions permitting, one shed can be made to serve several fields by siting it where they meet and removing the fencing there. Then, using gates or sliprails and fencing, a pen can be built around and at least 12ft (3.65m) from the shed, and any fields which may be resting or under treatment can be closed off.

Water sources

A healthy horse can need anything up to 12 gallons (55 litres) of water a day. Shortage of suitable water has a bad and most noticeable effect on the health and condition of any animal, so the supply must be ample, clean and from a source which the horse is not afraid to use freely. If he is frightened to approach because of rough or slippery ground,

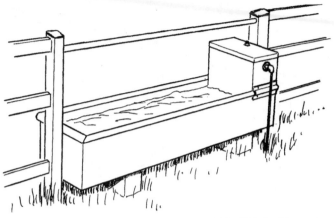

A trough positioned within a fence to serve two fields. If it had been set at an angle to the fence, it would have formed a dangerous projection into the field. The rail above will prevent horses from trying to jump over the trough, and this rail and the top fence rail should be level with the tops of the posts for safety. The pipe should ideally be lagged (below ground as well) and guarded with strong mesh or wooden boxing

low branches or sinking mud, or an unstable container, he will go without until forced, then snatch a quick sip to appease his immediate thirst.

A clear running stream with a stony or gravel bottom is good. A sand or earth bed, it is generally believed, can be sucked up with the water and eventually cause colic. A pond is unlikely to be clean enough, most being stagnant and with unsafe and unwelcoming approaches. In winter, there is the added danger of the horse's venturing on to the ice and falling in, so all ponds should be fenced off. If a horse prefers drinking muddy water to fresh, it is a sign he could be short of minerals in his diet. Ponds and streams should be checked regularly for pollution (consult the National Rivers Authority on analysis services).

If there is piped water to the field, an automatically-filling trough is good provided the mechanism is shielded from the horse and is not taken for granted but regularly checked to ensure it is filling up but not overflowing. These are available from agricultural merchants and stable fittings suppliers, in many cases. Plumbing should be well lagged to prevent burst pipes in winter. If the horses chew lagging above ground,

This post and rail fencing is safely constructed, with the rails on the inside, the bottom one a good distance from the ground, and the top rail level with the tops of the posts. The plastic dustbin, rammed into an old tyre, is a cheap, effective water container. It can be filled by hosepipe and is excellent in fields with no water supply laid on

pour old-fashioned bitter aloes over it – but not into the water! In winter, troughs and all water containers should have the ice broken at least twice a day as horses often seem unable to do this for themselves. If piped water ends in a tap over a water container, there should be some kind of smooth guard over and round the tap which enables humans to use it but keeps horses off, to prevent damage to both them and it.

If there is no piped water, a hosepipe will have to be run from a convenient tap to the field. Any water container, whether filled automatically, by tap or by hosepipe, should be smooth to prevent injuries. Sharp cornered troughs or tanks are dangerous, as can be the rims of old baths. Some metal containers, whether galvanised or not, contaminate the water with rust and rubber ones can make it taste horrible.

Plastic dustbins are good (the lids can be used as dung skeps). Choose the flexible type which will not crack should the horses bite them. Tie each bin to a support post in the fence (not where it will get leaves falling into it) with binder twine or rope round the top and middle and wedge the bottom into a close-fitting large rubber tyre for stability. Many tyre fitters are glad to sell these very cheaply. The advantages of water bins like these are that they are safe, easy to handle for scrubbing out, more than one watering point can easily be provided and they can be moved on a little way down the fence each day, preventing poached ground.

Safety

In rented fields one often comes across dangerous farm implements hidden in the grass which must be taken right out of the field, not just pushed to one side. Horses cannot be trusted to see and avoid even something as large as an old plough, and a chain harrow is easy for even us to overlook if the grass is more than a few inches long. Horses can canter right on to such things with serious consequences. Litter must be regularly checked for and removed, as should fertiliser sacks left lying about or blowing in from elsewhere.

Danger areas such as ponds should be fenced off. Even shallow ditches can be dangerous. Horses rolling near them can end up cast on their backs or sides in the ditch. They can die of exhaustion and shock just by struggling to get out, but if the dyke is deep and/or contains water, it is possible for a horse to drown.

Safety is largely a case of cultivating the habit of observation and imagination as regards the horses' field. Make a point of filling in holes with stones and earth, removing large rocks, loose or protruding tree roots (the tree has plenty more!), fallen boughs and dead (and therefore possibly dangerous) trees. Also make a habit of checking for and spotting damage to fencing, gates or shed every time you visit the field. Rest assured that if there is anything within reach of the horses which could cause them trouble, they will find it.

Security

Anyone keeping a horse out round the clock has to face the fact that one morning when they go to check on him he may not be there, and not because he might have escaped but because someone has stolen him. It is distressing but true that it is very easy to steal a horse from an open field in the dead of night. They are even stolen in broad daylight. But how do you make a field thief-proof? The answer is – you don't. All you can do is make life as difficult and discouraging as possible for the thief.

The first thing to be done is to get your horse freeze-marked. In Britain at present, there are a few companies offering this service, which is approved by the British Horse Society and police forces. The horse has a personalised number freeze-branded on his back. The super-chilled irons kill the pigment in the hair root and it grows back white, showing the number. With white or grey animals the hair follicle is killed completely by leaving the iron on a little longer, so the number is shown in bare skin. The horse is registered at the freeze-marking company's offices, and any freeze-marked horse stolen, or found away from home, is reported to the police, who check with the company for the name and address of the owner. Horses can be marked under the mane, if desired, although the number will not then be immediately visible at, for example, a sale. The marking companies normally offer rewards well above meat price for the recovery of the horse which act as incentives to sales operators and others to report such horses, and not slaughter or sell them. This system is much more effective than lip tattooing. Most companies provide stick-on or sew-on warnings for rugs and metal plates, to fix up in your yard, to the effect that the horses are marked.

The British army burns a code number on to its horses' hooves, and there is a company in Britain offering this service to civilian owners, using their post code. Not so visible as a freeze-mark on the back, it avoids the disfigurement by the latter (although it is under the saddle) and is preferred by many.

As for the field, it is highly impractical to make the fencing thief-proof or even thief-resistant. The best deterrent here is high, thick prickly fencing, which can take years to develop. Saws and wire-clippers will cope with most man-made fencing, unfortunately, but at least you can padlock your gates round the top and bottom hinges at each side so that they cannot easily be undone or lifted off the hinges.

It is a good idea to cultivate the favours of people living in the area and ask them to keep an eye out for strangers lurking around. Give them your telephone number (work and home) and ask that they contact you or some other designated person if anything suspicious is going on.

Breeding stock

Although this book is not specifically meant for breeders, some mention should be made of turning out breeding stock with other horses.

Much depends on the temperaments and personal relationships of the horses involved. If a broodmare's only companion is a friendly gelding, they will probably both be very miserable if separated just because 'the books' say the two do not mix. If a broodmare is turned out with an animal or animals which persistently chivvy her, and which might set on the foal if born when no human is about, it is obviously dangerous to leave her with them. Stallions are normally turned out alone, although, one hopes, within sight of other animals (when they are happy and balanced in their outlook). However, I have known of two stallions who each spent half of each day out in turn with an aged pony mare who kept them both firmly in their places and taught them manners. She would stand for no nonsense and would not let either of them even attempt to mount her and they both appeared extremely fond of her. They were both very well mannered towards their 'wives', too.

If animals which do not mix are to be turned out in adjoining fields, it is best to create a lane of double fencing between the fields. This could simply be done with electric fencing about 12ft (3.65m) away from one side of the fence, provided the horses are taught to respect it as described earlier.

Tethering

Tethering is a very poor way of keeping a horse at grass unless the horse fully understands what the tether is all about and will tie up peacefully, and is left tethered for only short periods to give a change of grazing. The horse must be tethered within easy reach of shelter and water, wear a well-fitting, supple headcollar or neckstrap round the throat and have a swivel on the end of the tether which ensures he cannot wrap his rope round and round the stake and end up with only a little ground. The stake must be firmly and deeply hammered into the ground, and the horse must not be tethered in dangerous surroundings or within reach of any enemies, from whom he will obviously be unable to escape.

The combined system

Although many horses live constantly at grass, there are undoubtedly times when it would be much better to be able to bring them in temporarily for convenience, say to facilitate preparation for some occasion; and it might become essential in times of illness or injury, so every effort should be made to obtain at least temporary use of a stable, perhaps by paying someone a small retainer rent to ensure availability when necessary. At a pinch, the field shed, if large enough, could have part of it safely sectioned off for the horse, although possibly the other animals might try to interfere with the occupant. Also, the 'prisoner' might try to get out to them.

The combined system of horse keeping means that a horse spends some of his time stabled and some outdoors and is really the best system of keeping any horse as it gives him and his owner the best of both worlds: the freedom of the outdoors and the comfort of a stable. When the land becomes unfit to use, usually when badly poached in winter, it may become essential to get the horses off it for at least part of the time and stable them, say, at night, or on summer days to get them away from sun and flies.

Another system of keeping them when the land is out of use, if the facilities can be arranged, is to bed down a large enough building, say a barn, large garage or implement shed, and construct a run or corral outside so they can wander freely in and out and stretch their legs while still having shelter. The surface of the run will have to be non-slip and not hard, or falls and injuries could occur. A covering of peat, sand or used bedding, even though it will get rained on, can make many surfaces acceptable if laid thickly enough. (This is yet another use for used bedding from stables or shed. If the practice is made of mucking out the droppings into one muck heap and the used bedding into another, the droppings will make highly saleable manure and the bedding can be used as described to good advantage.) A corral system such as this is far better for horses than either being cooped up in a stable with no exercise or relief from boredom when their field is out of use, or standing rooted in the mud of their paddock.

4 Grassland Management

It was not until I read an article on conservation some years ago that I realised just how important is grass, not only to horse owners but to the human race as a whole. Perhaps we do not grow grass to eat as we do cereal crops, but we grow it to feed animals on which we depend for food, whether they eat it in its natural growing form, as silage, hay or as processed cobs, cubes or meal. The article made the point that grass is our most neglected crop and the most underrated. Every year, millions of pounds worth of food potential is unrealised through neglect or mismanagement.

To the horse owner, particularly the owner whose horse spends most or all of his time in the field, good grass is a cheap, naturally balanced diet suited to the delicate equine digestive system. Even when meticulously managed, it is cheaper to provide than bought foods and definitely saves money in the long run. Those owners who have more than enough good grazing for their requirements need pay less attention to it than those who have barely sufficient. It is small acreages per horse which need most planning and care, because the smaller the area the more wear it gets. Pounding hooves and cropping teeth inevitably cover the same ground more often and the same amount of manure is dropped as on a larger field, so covering and contaminating with its smell (and probably worm eggs) a greater percentage of the available area.

Together, these three factors – hooves, teeth and droppings – combine to hamper seriously the growth of desirable grass on overstocked or neglected 'small' paddocks. I have placed the word 'small' in inverted commas because the size of the paddock matters less than the number of horses on it, eg while a 5 acre (2ha) paddock might be enough for two horses on a year-round basis, it would be cramped for three and definitely insufficient for four.

Many owners from a non-farming background have no idea what constitutes good or useless vegetation for grazing. To them, grass is just grass and they presume the horses will eat it willy nilly. Also, many of us have no real idea of how to care for what we have. To make matters more difficult, there is a difference between the sort of grass which is good for horses and that which is better for cattle.

Horses these days are normally required for athletic purposes – galloping, jumping, endurance work, trekking or hacking, or for breeding other horses able to do these things. They are expected to have a long, sound, useful life, unlike farm animals which are either used for the production of food (involving a fast growth and weight gain and a short life) or for producing other food animals; and their nutritional requirements and digestive processes and abilities are rather different.

Growth pattern and food content

Grass has 'waves' of growth, being more abundant and containing different levels of various nutrients at different times of the year. It contains most food value and protein in May and early June, which is nature's time when young animals are born and need food, and when lactating mothers need plenty of food to provide milk for this year's young and to nourish next year's offspring which is probably developing inside them. Stallions also need good food during the mating season to make fertile, healthy sperm.

From June onwards, the food value of grass gradually decreases. In early autumn, there is a flush of growth which, however, is not so rich in protein as spring grass, containing more carbohydrate, and by late autumn, there is often practically no nourishment left in the grass. It is almost all fibre. In very mild winters, grass may continue to grow slowly throughout the season and may contain more nutrients than usual, but this is still not enough to support an animal properly.

It has traditionally been believed that horses prefer short, young grass, but in fact they do graze any length of grass provided they find it palatable, and this is the crux of the matter. No matter how perfect, in theory, a grass is for horses, if they do not like it they will not eat it, and it will do them no good at all unless it finds its way inside them!

Because grass is such a variable food, its high food-value level in spring being possibly dangerous (particularly for animals which have a good deal of common or pony blood and which just cannot take much nourishment – this includes donkeys) and its nutritional value in winter virtually nil, we must learn when to restrict grass intake and when to supplement it with other food of a suitable type. Otherwise, the result could be a horse who is not only unfit to use through being unsuitably fed but possibly dangerously obese and suffering from laminitis, or conversely starved to emaciation or death through ignorance. Supplementary feeding and the recognition of condition (understanding when a horse is too fat or thin) are dealt with in Chapter 6.

It is nature's plan to provide plenty of food in the breeding season, tailing off the supply during the year. In winter, horses still eat grass from instinct but they will really be living off the reserves of fat they have built up in their bodies from good summer feeding (supposing they have been allowed to grow fat from ample food and a work-free summer). By spring, they will be noticeably lean and, indeed, the weaker animals will have starved to death before the spring grass appears. This illustrates the survival of the fittest, and shows nature ensuring that the weaklings are not around when breeding commences, to reproduce their weaknesses within the species. In domestication, of course, this sort of treatment is not only regarded as the height of cruelty (although it happens each winter) but as stupid from an economic point of view, as it surely costs more to build up a thin horse or replace a dead one than it does to keep an existing one properly fed.

Suitable grasses and herbs

It is not only the nutritional content of a grass which decides its value but also its physical characteristics, such as whether it has a long or short growing season (some grasses grow for only a few weeks, then die), whether it is palatable to the animals and whether it is strong enough to grow and tiller (spread) vigorously despite competition from other grasses and plants nearby. It should also be of a type which recovers quickly after grazing and which will persist in the pasture for several years without the necessity to keep reseeding the paddock.

It is advisable to include some grasses which appear early in the year and some which go on growing well into autumn, thus ensuring the field will be productive for a long season as when the early grasses have had their day the later ones will still have weeks of young, active growth left. It is important to top (mow) early grasses not grazed or they will smother the later ones.

For horses, whose hooves and teeth are particularly destructive to turf and grass, it is also advisable to have some hard-wearing turf-forming grasses (such as *Agrostis)* included in the mix to help form a resilient turf to protect the horses' feet and legs and the land itself. It is worth hand-sowing areas of these grasses in much-used areas which tend to become hard and bare in summer or badly poached in winter, eg along fences, in gateways and round troughs and shelters.

The climate and soil in your district will also determine what will and will not flourish under local conditions. Some grasses grow best in warm areas and others in cold; some prefer dry land and others damp. Formulating a seed mix is a job for an expert, and new species of grass are constantly being developed, and seed mixes formulated as research in this field continues.

It is well worth consulting, in the UK, the Equine Services Department of the Agricultural Development Advisory Service (part of your local Ministry of Agriculture, whose telephone number is available from your 'phone book or local reference library) or an independent consultant such as the Equine Management Consultancy Service, based at 20 Victoria Road, Bulwark, Chepstow, Gwent NP6 5QN, Wales.

The nutritionist at the firm whose seed mixes you are

considering should also be able to advise on a suitable mix for athletic horses, and if one doesn't exist ask if a mix can be made for you. Some firms will not want to bother, and may not have the knowledge. If you feel this is the case, or they try to sell you an alternative or substitute which is not tailor-made for horses, go elsewhere. These days there is no need to accept the sort of seed mix guaranteed to increase milk yields in cattle, for example, which will be almost sure to give your horse laminitis anyway. You want a mix which is for working horses, not the slightly 'richer' pasture with its different nutrient balance which is suitable for equine breeding stock – unless you are a breeder, of course. You have to be extremely careful over your seed mix if you keep native ponies and cobs. These animals were evolved to do well on the very sparse, low-energy, low-protein keep of unimproved land before the advent of agriculture, and must have a mixture made up accordingly if you do not have natural ranges for them. The type of land grazed by sheep is plenty rich enough for them.

The benefit of clover is often misunderstood, possibly because the term 'living in clover' is taken to mean contentment and luxury. Clover is valuable as it adds essential nitrogen to the soil whereas grass removes it, but too much clover will stifle the grass and, as it is rich in protein, could cause digestive and other troubles in horses. Another valuable property of clover is calcium, which is vital for all horses, not just breeding and youngstock. Limestone or chalky soils (high calcium) are traditionally best for rearing horses, but a deficiency in other soils can be corrected artificially by the application of lime and/or chalk, which also helps keep the land sweet. The calcium/phosphorous ratio should ideally be 1.5:1, giving more calcium than phosphorous, and the advice of a consultant should be sought before indiscriminately applying calcium, or indeed any other supplements, to your land for fear of doing more harm than good.

(Some years ago, I visited a famous stud near Lewes, at the foot of the Sussex Downs. The owner of the stud told me that the calcium from the Downs was constantly washed down on to the lower land in the area making it far too high in calcium so that he had to take retaliatory action by means of his horses' other feed. Apparently, the calcium also got into the drinking water, causing arthritis in human and animal occupants of the area, but because he closely controlled his horses' diets they did not suffer from arthritis – and some of them were very old – although he did!)

Apart from nitrogen and calcium in clover, there are also many important minerals not found in grass, so it can be seen that a balanced proportion of clover in horse pastures is a most important factor.

Herbs

Herbs, too, contain protein, plus calcium and minerals not available from grass alone, and should be included in all pasture seed mixes for horses, or sown separately if the pasture is otherwise in good order. The following herbs are suitable for horses: ribgrass, burnet, yarrow, sheep's parsley, dandelion and chicory, which is especially palatable. It is generally considered that clover and herbs together should comprise not more than one tenth of the whole pasture.

Horses' grazing habits

Horses designate sometimes quite large parts of their field as lavatories where they go to deposit droppings and urine. They do not contaminate the chosen dining areas as the smell of their own manure is repugnant to them, consequently the grass in the lavatory areas is ignored and wasted and that in the dining parts can become overgrazed and weakened. In practice, this means that parts of the paddock are constantly cropped down tight, even bare if the horses are left on long enough, while others are never touched. This in turn obviously implies that although you may have, say, a 4 acre (1.6ha) paddock, the actual grazing area may only be 3 acres (1.2ha). After a few weeks, a horse paddock begins to look uneven, showing short areas interspersed with areas of what looks, to the uninitiated, like plenty of lush grass remaining but what is really, in the horses' eyes, rank, contaminated grass, inedible even to hungry animals. Because these areas are receiving 'fertiliser' in the form of dung and urine, they become rich in plant nutrients excreted by the horses while the overgrazed parts become deficient in them, constantly giving and never receiving. This can eventually result in retardation of grass growth in the grazed areas and a practically unproductive paddock from a food viewpoint. A paddock in this state is called 'horse sick'. It is now that the owner's troubles can really start, because the horses become increasingly hungry. They chew the fencing, strip the trees and make themselves ill by trying out poisonous plants within their reach which they would probably normally ignore, or they can injure themselves trying to jump out to greener pastures in search of food.

The subject of the contamination of land by the smell of droppings was studied at the Equine Research Station (Animal Health Trust), Newmarket, England in the 1970s. It was found that even after using land over which ponies had established a grazing pattern for two or three arable crops, and then returning equines to it, the same areas were grazed as previously plus some not grazed before. By and large, the lavatory areas remained the same, however, so it would seem that the smell of the droppings persisted after all that time.

It was discovered, however, that liberally spreading the entire field with well-rotted farmyard (cattle) manure had the effect of disguising the smell, and when ponies were eventually returned a completely even grazing/dunging pattern resulted which persisted for many months afterwards. It appears that farmyard manure is valuable for horse paddocks not only because of the nutrients it provides but because it seems to mask the smell in the areas contaminated by equine droppings. The horses no longer find these areas offensive and so will graze there, thus putting to use land which was previously wasted.

Unfortunately, 'good old-fashioned' farmyard manure mixed with straw is becoming harder and harder to get as modern farming practices embrace the increasingly common (and to my mind appalling) policy of not giving the animals bedding, so all that is produced is slurry. When spread at normal rates this is regarded as far too potent for horse pastures. If you can somehow spread it thinly, or get hold of the 'real McCoy', I feel it would be worth while.

Many owners not unnaturally would like to use their own horses' manure on land, and it does seem that provided this is well rotted and over a year old the problem of contamination with smell does not occur. However, as so many owners now use shavings, it should be pointed out that shavings deplete the land of nitrogen so this would probably need carefully supplementing, under expert advice.

Parasites

The subject of internal parasites will be dealt with mainly in the next chapter, but some mention of them must be made here. Almost every horse and pony has worms to some extent, whose eggs and larvae are passed out in the droppings and so on to the pasture. The eggs hatch and the larvae crawl on to the grass, often quite some way from the droppings, to be eaten with the grass by grazing horses. Once inside the horses they mature, migrating through organs and arteries and causing sometimes fatal damage, finally establishing themselves in the intestines to suck the horses' blood, breed and begin the cycle over again.

It is known that consistent, frequent dosing (every four to six weeks) results in large numbers of parasites being killed and their breeding activities curtailed for this time, during which very few eggs and larvae are excreted. Therefore, with adequately-wormed horses, parasite infestation is not much of a problem.

It can be seen, however, how in horses *not* so wormed parasites can soon build up to dangerous levels, and good husbandry from this point of view alone would then demand that droppings were picked up regularly – as often as every day in warm, moist weather, the worms' optimal breeding conditions. The formerly recommended practice of spreading droppings in the lavatory areas to expose them to sun and air to desiccate and decompose them more quickly is not now recommended as it is felt that this will spread the larvae around before the sun kills them off. Every effort should be make to pick up droppings as often as possible (certainly where youngstock are grazing, and other breeding stock). However, hot sun and a dry atmosphere does kill many worm eggs and larvae, as does a sharp frost.

Cattle

Although it is possible to counteract the results of horses' grazing habits by mowing down the long grass and adding artificial fertilisers to the deprived areas, the results are not so good as another workfree and completely natural method – the use of cattle on the land.

Horses graze by cropping the herbage with their front teeth. They can and do take it right down to soil level, which is bad for pasture as it then takes weeks or even months to recover. They are also, as already mentioned, very selective in their diet and will leave much good grass if they do not happen to find it palatable, even when hungry. Cattle, however, obtain their grass by wrapping their tongues round it and tearing it off some way above the ground. They are physically unable to take it down to ground level and so are not able to feed off the areas overgrazed by the horses. Instead they eat the long parts the horses have left, being unoffended by the horses' droppings and also not so fussy over what they eat. They use for their lavatory areas, largely, the horses' grazing areas, thereby depositing much-needed nutrients there. When the horses return, after the short grass has grown again, they keep to their same pattern and graze in their previously selected areas, being similarly unoffended by cattle manure.

Cattle also play a valuable part in parasite control. As they graze in the areas containing the highest numbers of equine parasites, they will inevitably ingest them with the grass. Parasites cannot live in an unnatural host, and will be killed off. Likewise, any parasites of cattle eaten by the horses are also killed off, so each species again complements the other.

If nothing else were ever done to the land, the use of cattle alone would go a long way towards correcting the 'damage' done by horses. In most districts where there are horses, there are usually cattle nearby whose owners will normally be pleased to use your free grazing (I have never yet known a farmer who had enough land) at no cost to you.

Renovating and maintaining your land

If the land is your own or you have the use of it for some years, it is worth implementing a programme of drainage and reseeding (if necessary) and of subsequent fertilisation, treatment and use in order to get the best from it, whether the area is large or small. If you are unable to do the work yourself, a few enquiries among local farmers or a glance through your district's farming journals will produce either a farmworker or agricultural contractor who will do it for you.

The first step is to put right the drainage (for which you may be able to get a grant, especially if you are grazing cattle, too), if this has been advised. This is vital, as no methods of husbandry will work to good effect on badly drained land. It is best done in late summer or autumn as the grass is then past its best but the land should not be too wet for the work to be carried out.

To drain a field, tubular field-drains must be laid below the surface to collect the water and run it off into some suitable outlet, such as a ditch. Clay drains have been used for many years and last well, but a few years ago they began to be replaced by long plastic tubes which were felt to be easier and quicker to lay. However, in practice it has been found that these can crack too easily from the weight of soil above them, and whilst there is some return to clay drains, other materials are now being tried. Your field would be considerably disrupted by the work, as trenches have to be dug at intervals across the land, the drains inserted and the topsoil replaced, so it could be out of use for several weeks.

The second step is to rid the land of any unwanted herbage as far as possible. Spraying with herbicides should only be a last resort if the land is really bad, and then the clover and herbs will have to be replaced. It is much better in the long run to gradually get rid of what you do not want by persistent mowing down and uprooting, which in time will effectively kill off the unwanted growths. In this way, there is no risk of killing off valuable herbage or of having chemicals washed down into the land, with possibly deleterious side-effects on the soil or animals.

The third stage is heavy harrowing, a marvellous treatment for the land. A pitchpole harrow should be drawn across the field by Land-Rover or tractor twice both ways. This aerates the soil by loosening it and tearing out old roots, moss and dead, matted vegetation without going too far and destroying the precious protective turf, as does ploughing. (Once the land is back in use, it will do nothing but good if it is chain harrowed once each way each month throughout the growing season.)

Fourthly, whatever fertilisers have proved necessary should now be applied at the recommended rates. There are specific fertilisers such as lime, potash, calcium, phosphate and nitrogen, and general ones such as fishmeal or seaweed meal. It is important to follow the advice you have received on this subject, as a great deal of harm can be done to your land and horses by haphazard applications of just any product which sounds impressive in the advertisements. Some fertilisers can and should be applied frequently throughout the year while others are required only every few years. Any product which claims to produce a quick flush of protein-rich grass (eg straight nitrogen, pig or poultry manure) must be used with great care and a hay crop taken first before the horses are grazed, or serious digestive troubles can result.

Fifth, and finally, comes the sowing of your seed mix which, if possible, should be followed by rolling to consolidate the soil again. The only thing to do then is wait. After an April sowing, the land should be ready for you to begin using lightly in August or September, and after a July sowing, say, the following April or May.

Obviously, while the renovation programme is proceeding the horses must be kept off the land, mainly for their own safety but partly to avoid ruining the good work; it will, therefore, be necessary to section off the land, preferably into at least four parts (especially if reseeding with the subsequent waiting time involved) and renovate it piece by piece.

It is usually recommended that after the application of most fertilisers and weedkillers pasture should be left ungrazed for at least three weeks, unless there is a very heavy fall of rain, to ensure that the toxic properties have either become inactive or been washed away. Some products, though, are safe as soon as they are dry, but this point must be carefully checked with your adviser or veterinary surgeon.

Your land should be left until the grass has reached 4-5in (10-12cm) before being subjected to grazing, and at first should be grazed lightly. The following season, normal grazing in accordance with a sound management rota can be practised. Newly seeded paddocks should not be used for hay otherwise all the herbs, clover and fine-leaved grasses will be smothered and killed off. As mentioned earlier, the grass should be kept 'topped' to 3-4in (8-10cm) to allow these slow growers to establish.

A suggested management rota

A carefully thought-out rota is essential if the land is not to revert quickly to its former condition. The following routine is only a rough sample of what might be suggested for, say, an owner with two horses and 5 acres (2ha) of land. Precise details must depend on individual circumstances but the following might provide some guidelines at least.

If not already done, the land should be divided into three paddocks of roughly the same size (ensuring each has access to water and shelter facilities, which can be centralised as shown in the illustration on page 66. If one field is noticeably drier than the others it could be kept mainly for winter use and be sown with a good proportion of *Agrostis* or similar grasses to stand up to winter conditions. This field could also be used for exercising the horses (ridden or lunged) if required, so as not to spoil the others. The two 'summer'

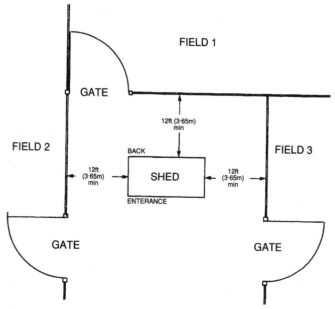

This shows how a field shed can be positioned to serve three fields. Two fields can be shut off for treatment and resting while the third is in use, and the horses can still get to the shelter

fields could have some early-growing grasses for early spring use, by which time the 'winter' field will be ready for its rest.

For convenience, let us call the winter paddock Field 1 and the others 2 and 3, and imagine that the rota has begun in spring, with the horses in Field 2.

When the grass in Field 2 begins to look uneven, with some short patches and some noticeably longer ones (in roughly three to four weeks) move the horses into Field 3. Ideally, now, Field 2 should be grazed by cattle for a week or so. Once they have gone, a few hours should be spent scything or mowing down any remaining long grass (preferably spreading it on to the over-grazed areas to rot down) and weeds. A light chain harrowing should now be given; then the field should be closed off to rest and grow.

When Field 3 begins to look patchy, move the horses back to Field 2. Field 3 now needs the cattle, mowing, harrowing and resting treatment, and by the time Field 2 is looking a bit ragged again, Field 3 will have recovered and be ready for use once more – and so the rota goes on.

From about mid-July on, Field 1 could be reintroduced into the rota, but should subsequently receive the 'treatment' and be allowed to grow during September before being put into sole use for the winter. At this time, Fields 2 and 3 should be grazed by cattle, mown, harrowed and given a good general fertiliser, before being shut up all winter. When the land is dry enough in spring, harrow these fields, and once the grass is making a good showing again they can be brought back into use as before. Field 1 should now be mown, harrowed thoroughly and fertilised, and shut up until midsummer.

It will be noticed that this rota allows a good deal of rest for each paddock, something most horse paddocks used for non-breeding stock rarely get. However, in order to keep land in good condition, at least three months' continuous rest is vital. With the type of system described, your land will repay you not only by looking pleasant but in the amount and quality of the grass it grows for your horses. The grass will be right for horses as opposed to dairy cattle so you should not have the problems of obesity and digestive troubles, including laminitis, so often associated with the latter, and in spite of the money you will have spent on it, and will continue to spend, it will still be a cheaper source of food by far than bought-in fodder and concentrates. Sick, neglected, overworked land is depressing to look at, bad for the horses' health and contentment and hard on your pocket in terms of reduced production and enforced supplementary feeding.

Compromises
It is quite possible to operate a successful rota with two fields. Even if you do not have enough land to enable the horses to receive considerable dietary support from the grass, do divide whatever you have into two and operate a rota as best you can, making up for the lack of grass by giving supplementary feeds. In such a case, try to rent some other suitable grazing for, say, six weeks during May and June and the same in September and October, as during these times the grass is growing and will have no chance to develop on

your own land if it is eaten off or trampled down as soon as it appears. If your land never gets a reasonable rest it will become useless for anything but exercise and you will have to buy almost all your horses' food. Such paddocks could each be given alternate winters off to ensure that they get their three months' continuous rest once in a while. Those who are able to obtain grazing only on a casual, fairly short-term renting arrangement, usually from farmers, are obviously extremely limited as to how they can manage the land, if at all. It is probably best to rent one field for spring and summer and one for autumn and winter, or, better still, one for each season, if possible, depending on the space available per horse.

Mixed grazing with cattle is perfectly acceptable and the two rarely bother with one another. The main points to check are, first, that the cattle should not be dairy cattle as they will almost certainly be on grazing too rich for horses, secondly, that they are free from ringworm which is contagious and can be difficult to cure and, finally, that they are hornless, otherwise a nasty accident could occur.

Making hay

It is always a temptation for horse owners to save money by taking a hay crop from their land, and this possibility can certainly be discussed with whoever you consult about your land. Mostly it is a waste of time and money unless the land can comfortably be spared and the crop is certain to be well made and of high quality. Specialist knowledge is needed to know when a crop is ready for cutting (most are left much too late until past their best) and to judge the weather if the crop is to be field dried. Expensive machinery is also needed unless you are going to scythe and truss it by hand – to the benefit of the crop, I might add! Even if you engage a contractor to do the work, it is unlikely he will be free to come at a few hours' notice when you judge your crop to be in its prime for cutting or baling, and a few hours can make a big difference to a crop, let alone a few days.

Unless you can overcome all these problems, I feel it more

satisfactory and economical to feed your grass growing and buy the best hay you can find.

Poisonous growths

A good deal is written about poisonous plants and trees, but in fact genuine cases of plant poisoning are rare. The trouble mainly arises in hungry animals because poisonous things are usually bitter tasting and normally only eaten when horses become desperate enough to experiment with almost anything. The moral here is obvious – if you do not have enough grass to keep your horses content, give them supplementary food (probably hay or hayage – see Chapter 6) so that they are not forced to satisfy their hunger on lethal vegetation.

It is not always easy to know what is poisonous and what is not as some poisonous plants look like others which are harmless or actually beneficial. Short of a practical lesson from an expert, the best most of us can do is learn from books and compare the descriptions with any unfamiliar growths in our own fields. It is no good renting a field only to find out too late that it is full of ragwort.

Two common poisonous trees to watch for are laburnum and yew. Yew, apparently, is not bitter tasting but quite deadly. Short of chopping down the trees, the best solution is to put fencing round them several yards further away than might seem necessary, so that there is no chance of the horses' reaching them. Many garden plants are poisonous, also shrubs, two common ones being laurel and rhododendron. Other common plants which are poisonous to a greater or lesser degree, some when alive, some when dead and some both, are: acorns, conkers, plants of the nightshade family, thorn apple, some privets, hemlocks, horse and marestails, buttercups, aconite, foxgloves, dodder, bryonies, some types of bracken, old man's beard, mature charlock and potato plants.

Garden cuttings can also be dangerous to horses, and lawn clippings can cause fatal colic by fermenting in the intestines and rupturing them. If the intestines do not actually rupture, the excess gas from the fermentation will cause considerable pain and the poisons will cause illness. Horses should be kept well away from compost heaps, therefore.

Poisonous plants thrive on neglected, sour land, by ditches and ponds and under hedgerows. There are specific sprays and treatments available, with new ones coming out all the time, and your local branch of the Ministry of Agriculture can give up-to-date advice on this, as can your veterinary surgeon or pasturage consultant.

As with other unwanted vegetation, it is better to spray only as a last resort if the land is really bad, it being preferable constantly to mow down, uproot and remove the plants, which are often equally poisonous when dead and also more appealing, as they then often lose their bitter taste. Dead plants should, therefore, be cleared out of the field and burnt. All animals must be removed while these processes are going on, and not put back until all chemicals are inactive, the exact safety margin depending on the product used.

A full dissertation on the subject of poisonous plants would be too long for this book, but an excellent publication is available from local offices of Her Majesty's Stationery Office or through the Ministry of Agriculture, Fisheries and Food. This is Bulletin No 161 *British Poisonous Plants*.

Ragwort

Special mention should be made of this plant as it is very common, very poisonous and very difficult to eradicate permanently. Furthermore, the Ministry of Agriculture is empowered under the Weeds Act of 1959 to enforce owners of infested land to clear it, although this rarely seems to happen judging by the spread of the plant in recent years. Ragwort (and there are various types) grows to a height of 2-3ft (60-90cm), with a straight, ribbed stem and dark, ragged-looking leaves. The flowers resemble large, bright yellow daisies growing in umbrella-like clusters. Ragwort thrives on land which is horse sick or neglected. It is stifled on well-managed land with a close-knit, ample sward.

Its alkaloid poisons act mainly on the liver. They accumulate (not being excreted) and in trying to render them harmless some of the liver cells die, being replaced by fibrous (cirrhotic) tissue. The liver does not work to full capacity anyway, and a few cells at first are not missed. But as the poison builds up from repeated grazing, or if a lot of poison is suddenly ingested at once, the liver becomes progressively destroyed by which time treatment is often pointless and mostly aimed at relieving discomfort. The healing process of the liver may take days, weeks or even months, depending on the amount of ragwort eaten. Just a few plants may cause great illness. The symptoms are varied as the liver is a vital organ performing many different functions, and it is advisable to consult your veterinary surgeon on this point. He is the person to tell you what signs to watch for.

There are now weedkillers to treat ragwort but it is necessary to spray yearly for several years as the plant is a perennial. Spraying, if decided upon, should be carried out in the 'rosette' stage, ie when the leaves are flat on the ground, and just before the flowering head begins to come up. The leaves then wither quickly and the paddock is fit to use quite soon. Plants *can* be sprayed up to the early bud stage but large plants need removing as they take too long to really rot away.

In practice, ragwort is not generally eaten when growing as it is most unpalatable, but *is* eaten when wilted or dry as its bitter taste then disappears. It should be stressed again that ragwort plants in a dead or dying condition – sprayed, cut down or uprooted – *must* be scrupulously picked up and taken right out of the field well out of reach of horses, not just dumped on the other side of the fence. They should preferably be burnt to avoid accidental access. If such plants are left within reach of horses they are almost bound to be eaten.

In addition to spraying, hand pulling is recommended, when the flower head is long enough to get a good grip, and uprooting with the aid of a garden fork, as a constant practice throughout the growing season. Get into the habit of taking a sack and a fork with you whenever you go into a paddock supporting ragwort. Although the plant has an extensive rootstock and will shoot from a tiny fragment left in the ground, constant uprooting is really the only way to get on top of it, and will eventually eliminate it altogether.

Readers are advised to obtain a copy of *Pasture Management for Horses and Ponies* by Gillian McCarthy, published by Blackwell Scientific Publications. This detailed, authoritative and very readable book is the standard work on the subject. It is very helpful, informative and practical and an essential source of information on a subject which is of vital concern to owners of outdoor horses.

5 Health and Condition

As the owner of your horse, you are responsible for his health and well-being. He is totally dependent on you for providing him with the necessities of life such as food, water and shelter, and for maintaining him in good health. It is also the owner's responsibility to provide veterinary care when the horse is sick or injured.

A great asset for anyone involved in caring for horses is the possession of a good, up-to-date veterinary book. In recent years, veterinary research has progressed considerably in several fields and although a veterinary surgeon is always the person to consult in matters of health and who will have access to the most recent knowledge and ideas in his field, reading at least one veterinary book on horse health matters will equip you with good basic knowledge of the afflictions to which your horse can succumb and of the type of injuries he can sustain (and these are many in such an athletic animal). Equally important, you will gain knowledge of how your horse's body functions in normal health. If we do not know what is normal, how shall we know what is abnormal?

Finding a suitable veterinary surgeon

Although all veterinary surgeons receive the same lengthy training, some prefer to specialise in certain fields after qualification. There are veterinary practices which deal with all types of animal, some only small animals, some large animals and some specialising in only one type of animal. Although any veterinary surgeon could adequately treat your horse, it is logical that one who has chosen to specialise in horses, or at least in large animals, will naturally have more interest in them and so probably be more up-to-date in their treatment than one wishing to work with only dogs for example. You can learn from other horse owners which practices deal with horses and which specialise in them, and choose from one reasonably near where you keep your horse. If you suddenly find your horse with a broken leg in the field, you will need help from a vet based two or three miles away, not from one working five or ten miles away. It is important that you have a veterinary surgeon you can talk to. Vets always seem to be extremely busy, but it is a disadvantage to have one who, because of lack of time, does not explain exactly what is wrong with your horse or what treatment he is having.

Veterinary surgeons' charges are usually reasonable when set against their long training, the hazardous nature of their work and their level of knowledge and skill. The main charges will be for drugs, treatments and travelling expenses. It is my experience that veterinary surgeons liberally give out advice free, especially to their regular clients, and your vet's advice will be one of your greatest assets in maintaining your horse's health.

A yearly care-plan

Have a talk with your vet and explain what you are going to do with your horse. Any horse in work should have a yearly medical check to make sure he is still likely to be able to perform the work you require of him. Heart, lungs, eyes, action and many other things will be taken into account. Blood tests can be carried out to check various aspects of the horse's metabolism, plus urine tests and anything else which your vet feels will be of use.

An annual routine should be worked out for vaccinations (mainly against influenza and tetanus) and for the administration of anthelmintics (worming medicines). Teeth also need periodical checks, every six months in youngsters, possibly once a year in older horses. Organise a routine and get several jobs (and maybe several horses) done at the same time, which will save on visit/travelling expenses. A suitable time for vaccinations should be carefully planned. Although it is normally better to vaccinate horses against influenza shortly before a busy season is about to begin, when they will be frequently exposed to the disease due to travelling, many owners find that their animals go slightly off colour after vaccination, so time must be allowed for any recovery necessary. Vaccinations are normally needed every six months in horses frequently exposed to influenza and once a year or even every two or three years for tetanus. These are matters on which your vet can advise.

Signs of health and disease

Anyone closely connected and working with a horse on a regular basis will get to know that animal very well unless he or she is insensitive. When a person also cares greatly about an animal, the chances of reaching a deep relationship and understanding with it are considerably increased, and so are the chances of noticing, or even just feeling intuitively, when something is amiss. Maybe it is just a look in the horse's eye, or perhaps it is something more noticeable. Whatever it is, no one will ever get to know your horse like you do, and it is you who will probably be the first to notice something wrong. It is also to you that your vet will look for information about your horse when normal. Many a time I have been asked by a vet: 'Are his glands swollen?' (when the vet has been standing right next to the horse), 'Does he always stand like that?' or 'Does he usually stay lying down when you go to him?' This is because the owner is more likely to know the answer to such questions than the vet. Each horse's make, shape and action is slightly different, and its behaviour can be very individual indeed. So we must study and really get to know our horses in order to help our veterinary surgeons as much as possible.

Some physical signs

A horse in good health will have a general appearance of 'bloom' about him, even when filthy with wet mud. His coat should have a certain sheen to it and, even in winter, lie close to the skin. If it is dull and 'staring' (ie the hair is standing stiffly away from the skin) the horse is probably either very cold or in poor health. He should have an alert, interested expression, unless sleepy, and should take note of his surroundings. Any horse which takes little notice of humans or other horses or who isolates himself, standing apart in the field, could well be sick. Even if he is the herd outcast, he will linger about on the fringes of the herd seeking company by instinct when well.

Horses rarely lie down flat out for more than half an hour; if they do, suspect trouble. Lying down excessively, in any position, should be noted, particularly if the horse also seems dull and withdrawn. When horses lie down to roll they very often do one side first, get up and then do the other side. After this they should have a good shake. Rolling without shaking afterwards can be a sign of internal disorder, particularly if done often.

The horse's eating and drinking habits should also be watched although this may not be easy in an outdoor horse. Take the time to stay and observe him for several minutes. If the horse appears to be eating and swallowing normally this is often a general sign of good health, but note whether he takes in and chews food, then drops it out of his mouth again in lumps, or whether food is coming back down his nostrils with saliva. The latter could be a sign that his gullet is blocked (known as 'choke') either from chewing wood (fencing or shelter) and swallowing pieces or from being given dry food. Dropping food out of the mouth ('quidding') is a sign of worn and sharp teeth causing pain and preventing the horse from chewing his food properly.

If you can manage it by being close to your horse for long enough, note whether he seems to be drinking very often or hardly at all, as both are signs of possible disorder. It is difficult to check this in a grass-kept horse, however. When several horses are kept together, it is also difficult to know if the water level in a non-automatic container is going down because some are drinking too much and others not enough, or whether they are all normal, so try to watch them all and get to know their habits. Self-fill containers, obviously, although saving a lot of work, are no help at all in enabling owners to check consumption. Check also that no horse is being kept off water, food or shelter by more dominant companions. If so, the best answer is usually to remove the

The spot under the jaw where the pulse can be taken

bully to another field, but it may be necessary to find somewhere else for the harrassed horse.

Getting to know your horse's normal temperature, pulse and respiration rates can also be a big help. The horse's normal temperature will be around 100.4°F (38°C), and his at-rest pulse rate between 32 and 40 per minute with breathing about 12 per minute. As your grass-kept horse will be almost constantly on the move, these rates will be varying all the time, but if you try to get initial readings at the same time, under the same conditions every day for a week, you will at least have some idea of what is normal for him. If you are in the habit of standing your horse in a stable regularly, say to prepare him for work or some other care procedure, he will be used to this and could well relax and give you more accurate readings. If he is not used to it, however, he could become upset by it, which will send up his pulse and respiration rates.

To take a horse's temperature, buy a stubby-ended thermometer from your vet and ask him to show you how to shake down the mercury to below 90°F (32°C) before use. Moisten or grease the end and, holding it by the top, insert it into the horse's rectum (holding his tail to one side towards you) with a gentle side-to-side twisting motion. Leave it in place for a minute or half a minute, depending on the time stated on it, and read off the temperature.

To take a horse's pulse always use your fingers (not your thumb which has a pulse of its own) where a main artery passes over a bone. The most common spot is inside the jawbone just under the rounded bone, as shown in the illustration on page 77. Other places are inside the elbow a few inches down, and under or alongside the dock about a hand's breadth from the root of the tail. This latter spot has the advantage that you can take the horse's temperature at the same time. Feel around with your fingers and press so that you are sure you have got the pulse. Count for half a minute (you will obviously need a watch with a second hand), double the count and you have his rate per minute.

To take a horse's respiration, stand just behind and to one side of him where you can see the outline of his opposite flank, ie stand on his left and watch his right flank. Watch for the rise and fall of the flank, sometimes difficult to spot, especially in a fit horse, and count each lift and fall as one breath. Again, count for half a minute and double the count.

When horses are standing and resting, they often rest one hind leg alternately, and occasionally a foreleg, too, changing over from time to time. If a horse persistently rests the same leg, suspect trouble in that leg, even if he is not actually lame.

A horse's droppings, the remnants of his food once it has been digested, will also give a good guide to his state of health. Grass-kept horses' droppings are moister and greener than stabled horses', but they should still form into recognisable balls which break easily on hitting the ground. If they are sloppier or much harder than this, the horse could have some digestive disorder.

The horse's general demeanour will tell you a lot, not only whether he is well but also whether he is unhappy out at grass. If he stands with a forlorn expression, head down, ears back and tucked up (pinched looking in the hip/belly region), he could be ill or generally unhappy. In winter, this, perhaps combined with shivering, is a sure sign that the horse is cold and miserable. Horses can stand below-freezing temperatures quite happily if the weather is still, and dry, especially if it is sunny. Indeed, they seem to find such weather conditions exhilarating, as do many humans and other animals. It is when cold is combined with wind and/or wet that they begin to suffer most and seek shelter. The horse's natural winter coat insulates him quite well normally, holding a layer of body-warmed air within it all round the skin. When the wind disturbs this hair and lets out the warm air, the horse obviously feels cold, and when rain or snow wet the coat it clings together, flattens and cannot hold the layer of warm air. The wet in itself accentuates the effects of wind and cold.

Those animals with naturally thick coats (cold-blooded or heavy-weight types or those with a lot of cob or pony blood) stand such conditions better than the shorter, finer coated warm-blooded and hot-blooded types, which originate in warm climes and do not have the inherent protection against the British climate. It is usually such horses who benefit most from a New Zealand rug (see Chapter 7). Some people maintain that these rugs destroy the warm-air layer by flattening the coat, and this is true, but the rug itself is both windproof and waterproof, and *some* air will remain under the hair. Generally, when well maintained, these rugs have more advantages than disadvantages.

The horse's skin and coat are an excellent guide to his condition, a supple, movable, glossy covering to his body being indicative of good health and also providing a weather-resistant protection for him. Feeding a higher fat diet, most conveniently by adding soya oil or corn oil to each feed in amounts recommended by a vet or nutritionist (probably about a dessertspoonful (10ml) in each feed), does help improve the condition of skin, hair and hooves, as does adequate methionine, biotin, MSM and calcium in the diet, maybe by means of supplementation. Linseed oil can be used but if you opt for this make sure it is the type for animal feeding, not that used by decorators and artists for cleaning brushes, which is poisonous.

Some specific disorders

There are many disorders which can affect horses, of course, and the study of one of the previously-mentioned veterinary books will familiarise you with most of the more common or serious ones, plus usually giving you a good deal of information about the horse's general physiology. In this section, I should like to give some basic information on conditions likely to affect outdoor horses more than stabled ones so that owners can be particularly on the lookout for them.

Laminitis
see under Feet and Shoes, page 88.

Mud fever/rain rash
These two conditions are caused by the same organism, *Dermatophilus congolensis*, which attacks the skin when weakened by constant wetting. Rain rash is as common in warm, humid conditions as in cold weather, but mud fever usually seems to occur most in colder conditions.

Mud fever can be initially noticed by the heat it causes in the skin, so owners should regularly feel their horses' legs (particularly white socks) for warmth. The condition usually starts up the back of the pasterns but can spread knee- or hock-high in fine skinned or susceptible individuals. The organism causes inflammation and great soreness, scabbing and swelling of the affected limbs, with chapped, cracked skin oozing yellow pus. It lives between the scab and the skin, so part of the treatment is to remove the scabs and expose the 'bugs' to the air. If the scabs are very hard and secure and the legs painful, it may be necessary to administer an anaesthetic to do this job, or the scabs can be softened with sulphanilamide powder creamed in water and mixed with castor oil. Whatever treatment is prescribed by your vet (and it is definitely a job for a vet), he or she will almost certainly tell you to bring the animal in and get its legs thoroughly dry, for obvious reasons, so stabling will have to be arranged. Horses can transfer the infection to their muzzles if they bite their legs, or to their bellies when they lie down.

Rain rash, although rarer and usually less serious, is a similar condition occurring on the shoulders, back, loins and quarters during very rainy weather. The skin becomes sore, the scabs cause the hair to look tufty (a characteristic appearance) and with both rain rash and mud fever, raw (not just bare) skin will result at some point, and maybe re-scabbing in bad cases. Dermatophilus infection can be very unpleasant and painful for the horse, especially on the legs, and can certainly put the horse off work. Treatment of bad cases can be long drawn out so alert vigilance on the part of the owner is essential.

Thrush
see under Feet and Shoes, page 92.

Allergies to chemicals/fertilisers/plants
Skin allergies to products used on the land or blown over from neighbouring land can occur and cause unpleasant skin conditions. Some of these occur on the muzzle and white socks, sensitive areas constantly in contact with the grass and soil, and take the form of blistering, cracked, peeling skin and swelling with soreness. Animals with liver disease can become sensitised to some plants, contact with which causes white areas to become reddened and sore. Allergy to pollen, especially from oilseed rape, causes COPD symptoms in susceptible horses in summer.

Removal of the cause is at the root of any treatment of allergies, so it may be necessary to remove the affected animal to other grazing. Not all animals in a field may be affected, allergies being as individual in horses as in humans. Veterinary treatment should be applied according to the condition prevailing, as these symptoms often do not subside just because the causative factor has been removed.

Parasites
A great deal is spoken of worms and other parasites, and it is true they do cause a great deal of unthriftiness, illness and even death.

The most common internal parasites are ascarids (mostly

affecting young animals) and strongyles (redworm) which cause serious trouble in mature animals. Outdoor horses are particularly susceptible to infection with every bite they take, being permanently exposed to infection, unlike stabled animals which spend a good deal of time away from the source of infection, unless they eat infected bedding.

The life-cycles of parasites vary, but generally they begin with eggs and worm larvae being passed out in the droppings on to the pasture. Eggs and larvae are both microscopic so it is no use poking about in the droppings trying to spot them. Even adult worms are difficult to see.

In warm, moist weather, eggs will hatch within twenty-four hours and the larvae crawl on to the surrounding grass, sometimes for quite long distances, where they can be eaten by some unsuspecting horse and regain access to his intestines. Ascarid larvae migrate through the horse's lungs, often causing coughing and runny noses in young horses; strongyles do more damage by migrating through the blood vessels, often congregating at certain points in vast numbers, causing damage to the arteries (aneurisms or 'ballooning'). Usually, it is arteries serving the intestinal tract which are affected, causing the blood supply to a certain part of the tract to be cut off, with the result that the area dies off causing a very serious problem for all concerned. This is why worms are said to cause colic in horses, as the horse will show typical colic signs (pawing the ground, biting the flanks, rolling and lying on the back) in such cases.

Treatment of ascarids and strongyles, and so prevention of the above horrendous problem, is quite simple and effective. The trouble is that infection starts very early in life, as a foal first begins grazing, and if worm-control methods on the stud were less than exemplary a good deal of damage will already have been done to the horse's body by the time the larvae eventually migrate back to the intestines, hook their teeth into the lining (causing more damage), suck the horse's blood and begin laying eggs to start the process all over again.

Modern thinking indicates that horses should be treated for worms every four to eight weeks, depending on conditions prevailing. Obviously, in small fields or on overstocked land which never sees anything but horses, never has the droppings picked up and is never rested, the infection levels will be much higher than in well managed land (as discussed in Chapter 4). Your veterinary surgeon will advise on suitable treatments and drugs.

Counts of eggs and larvae in droppings can be made to ascertain what species are present and in what levels, but the results are unreliable as the worms' egg-laying and 'passing-out parades' are erratic.

The worms do become resistant to drugs after a time, so it is normally recommended that drugs from different groups are used alternately to help prevent this. There is, however, a school of thought which believes that frequent switching of drugs introduces the worms to them all and that they will, therefore, become resistant to them all. As usual, the vet is the person to discuss this with. At present, no resistance has been reported to the drugs pyrantel and ivermectin (zimecterin in USA). The use of ivermectin has made parasite control even easier and more effective as it will also kill migrating larvae at single dosage rates, vastly reducing the numbers of larvae returning as mature adults to the gut. Livery owners whose horses are out with those of owners who do not worm their horses properly are advised to use ivermectin to keep their individual horses' infection levels down, as otherwise they will significantly reinfect themselves with every bite of their infested pasture.

Dosing a horse at grass is just as easy as dosing a stabled one, as the relevant drug can simply be squirted in paste form from a safe and handy plastic syringe on to the back of his tongue. Some crafty horses wait, holding the paste in their mouths, and spit it out when you are not looking, so try to get the paste back far enough and give your horse some relished titbit afterwards to make sure he has swallowed.

Tapeworm
There has been an increased incidence of tapeworm infestation in horses in recent years so ask your vet to also check for this. A double dosage of the drug pyrantel will take care of tapeworm, normally in early winter.

Lungworm

Unfortunately for donkeys, they have received a bad press in the past as harbourers of lungworm and as the source of passing them on to horses. They are not so badly affected as horses, who often develop coughing and unthriftiness when infected.

Again, the larvae are picked up from pasture and migrate to the lungs to mature. The eggs they lay pass up the horse's throat (whether he is coughing or not), are swallowed down into the intestinal tract and passed out on to the pasture, and so it goes on. Usually, in horses, the larvae do not mature but just remain to cause trouble as immature forms, so if a horse at grass begins coughing, suspect lungworm and call the vet for advice and treatment.

Bots

These are not worms but the larval stage of the bot fly, which lays its eggs on the horse's legs in the summer. The horse licks them off and swallows them, and they hatch out in the stomach, clinging to its lining and causing tissue damage and indigestion. It is for this reason that many vets recommend using a worm medicine effective against bots as well as ascarids and strongyles in the autumn and winter months, to expel the larvae from the stomach.

From the above descriptions of parasites and their misdoings, it can be understood why it is constantly recommended that droppings are picked up from horse pastures very frequently (every day in warm weather) as this is one sure way of keeping down infestation. Unfortunately, this is highly impractical for some owners, particularly those who have to hold down a job as well as care for a horse. Cattle (and, less usefully, sheep) grazing the field do eat some of the larvae, but one quick and sure way of killing adults and larvae inside the horse, or so seriously debilitating them that they cease egg-laying for several weeks, so not infecting the droppings, is to treat horses every four to eight weeks with an effective drug on the advice of a vet. If using ivermectin the time between dosing can usually be increased.

Every horse on the pasture should be done on this basis as just one infected horse can seriously affect the health of the others and nullify their owners' attempts to keep them worm-free.

Flies and other insects

Flies, although not strictly parasites, do cause considerable distress to horses, as described earlier in this book. Inflamed, swollen eye membranes, jarred legs from galloping and constantly harried and exhausted horses are the results of fly-strike in summer. Warble flies, now more or less eradicated, lay eggs on horses' legs, the larvae from which hatch out, burrow under the skin to the back and cause hard, painful lumps there. The culicoides midge is responsible for a very distressing condition known as sweet itch, which is brought on by a horse's allergic reaction to the saliva of this biting midge. The areas most affected are around the withers and tail, the severe itching making the horse rub himself raw and compounding his distress. As the midge is most active for the first two or three hours after dawn and the last two hours or so before sunset, it is often recommended that horses are brought in then, which does help.

It does not help the owner of a grass-kept horse, however, and although there are various methods of relieving the distress, surely the best treatment of sweet itch and other fly-related disorders is to prevent the insects landing to do their damage in the first place. This is comparatively easy to do by using a really effective fly repellant on the horse. There are various types available from saddlers and veterinary surgeons, also agricultural merchants, but the best come into the category of 'residual' repellants, which state clearly that they are effective for a certain number of days (usually a week). Other types are only effective for a few hours, if that, and are not sufficient for a horse out all the time (some insects fly at night, too).

Check with your vet (yet again) on the best type or make to use, and follow instructions faithfully. Usually use of these products must begin in spring before flies get bad, so their effects build up on the horse and provide a really effective invisible 'shield'. If the horse sweats a lot, or the weather is wet, they will have to be applied more often but, even so, they do work. If your horse objects to aerosol sprays (which most do) apply the product on a rag. Most residual products have to be mixed with water and applied with a rag or sponge anyway. The help and comfort these products give to outdoor animals really are considerable and I strongly recommend their use. A fly-fringe on the headcollar gives some help to sensitive eyes, too.

Lice

Apart from worms, almost every horse or pony at grass will be infested by lice to some degree, normally during cooler weather as this most favours their development. They are tiny yellowy-brown insects which bite the skin to suck blood, causing intense itching and rubbing in the horses affected. Lice spread from one horse to another as they rub against each other and the rubbing and biting which occur result in bald, scurfy areas of skin. The louse population on any one horse can build up very quickly but effective shampoos and powders, available from your vet, will clear up the condition.

In bad cases, as the horse will probably have a winter coat at the time infestation is worst, it is necessary to clip off the hair in the affected areas (usually the neck, shoulder and forward part of the back) so the horse may have to be stabled due to the loss of his coat. The clipped hair should be burnt to kill the lice which may otherwise infest other animals, and the affected horse's clothing (including New Zealand rug) must be treated as well.

Ringworm

This is a fungal infection which horses can catch from one another, from cattle and from fields, fences and shelters (and, obviously, clothing and grooming kit) with which infected animals have been in contact. The spores remain active for many months, so proper treatment of the disease is essential. Small crusty bald patches of skin are the giveaway, caused by the hairs breaking off at their bases, and can appear anywhere on the body.

Apart from the antibiotic griseofulvin which can be given in the feed, two new treatments (at the time of writing) can be applied to the areas infected and also to clothing, buildings, grooming kit and anything with which the horse comes in contact. These treatments are Imaverol and Mycophyt. Horses can develop a degree of immunity to ringworm fungi of the same type so if a particular kind is prevalent in an area resistance to it could develop.

Grass sickness

Grass sickness, which affects only grass-fed animals, is a well-known disease now reported all over Britain. Research has been extensive, and some hope is now emerging that we shall soon understand the cause and prevention, although it is still usually incurable and nearly always fatal. Horses can graze fields known to be affected and, presumably because they develop resistance to the causative agent, remain well and healthy, but when a new horse is introduced to that field it becomes ill very quickly.

During the course of the disease, the nerves supplying the digestive system become damaged and the stomach and intestines simply stop working – sometimes the horse is even unable to swallow – and fill with a green liquid to the extent that they burst. The pressure of the full stomach on the diaphragm compresses the blood vessels supplying the heart, and the horse can die in shock. Sometimes animals die within hours or days, sometimes it takes weeks or months, but the horse always suffers greatly.

Symptoms of grass sickness are inability to swallow and general colic symptoms of pawing the ground, repeated rolling or lying down and getting up again, biting the flanks, lying on the back and a general air of great discomfort and pain. Any symptoms resembling the above in grass-kept horses should cause owners immediately to call the vet to diagnose exactly what is wrong.

Before taking on new land for grazing your horse, sound out everybody in the area as to the incidence and localities of the disease and never graze your horse in a field known to have had a grass sickness case on it. It is worth adding that every opportunity should be taken to support research into the cause and treatment of grass sickness.

Feet and shoes

The feet of a grass-kept horse often need considerable attention even if unshod, as the horn is constantly exposed to wet conditions for much of the year, and to hard, and possibly rough, ground at other times. Horses with healthy horn should not cause too much trouble, but those with poor quality horn are often subject to chipping and cracking in summer and to softening and easier wearing away in winter. Sometimes the bulbs of the heels wear badly, too.

Generally, soya or corn oil added to the feeds and adequate amounts of methionine, biotin, MSM and calcium, maybe in a supplement or specialist feed such as alfalfa (lucerne), will greatly help in time, but as it can take about six months for horn to grow from coronet to ground, badly affected feet will need help from an expert farrier to get them over the waiting period. Of course, the farrier's services will be needed approximately every six weeks for trimming, and shoeing if the horse is working, in any case, but you could need him more often if the horse is experiencing foot problems. The farrier can best cope with cracks in the feet, broken (and probably unbalanced) feet and soft horn by judicious shoeing, nail placements, shoe choice and other, surgical procedures.

If the horse is to be without shoes (and this is quite feasible even for a working horse if most of his work is on soft ground) the feet should be trimmed and balanced and well rounded off to help minimise chipping and cracking. Rounding off is only done slightly and cannot be equated with that heinous crime, dumping, in which the toe is shortened to fit the shoe instead of the shoe being made to fit the foot.

If the horse is to be shod for the sake of protecting his feet, lightweight race exercise plates may be quite adequate. If your farrier feels he needs a broader webbed (wider) shoe for added protection, he may fit a conventional lightweight

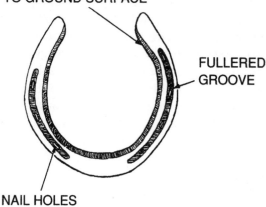

CONCAVED OUTWARDS
TO GROUND SURFACE

FULLERED
GROOVE

NAIL HOLES

A concaved, fullered hunter shoe (without calkin or wedge) suitable for general wear. The concave shape lessens suction in mud and the fullering provides better 'grip' on the ground surface

hunter shoe without the wedge on the outer heel. These shoes are concaved on the inner edge so that they are wider where they touch the foot (the bearing surface) than on the surface which touches the ground. They are also 'fullered out', which means the ground surface is not flat (known as a 'plain web' shoe) but has a recess running around the shoe on the ground surface presenting an upward groove. This means the surface which touches the ground is, in fact, two narrow ridges of metal. This pattern of shoe gives greater grip on the ground surface while reducing suction from mud, which can pull off a shoe and tear the foot in wet conditions. It also lightens the shoe for horses in active work.

It is best to discuss your horse's living conditions, feet and work with your farrier, and decide between you how best to shoe him (if at all) and care generally for his feet. You should, in any case, keep a daily eye on the state of his feet and shoes. The feet should be picked out and checked at least once a day for wedged-in stones, worn or loose shoes, risen clenches and cracking or softening horn, and appropriate action taken.

Kicking

If several horses share a field and a kicking match develops, serious injury can be inflicted by shod hooves. For this reason, many outdoor horses are shod only in front (the forefeet carrying more of the horse's weight and, so, being in greater need of protection). Inveterate kickers are a curse and, for the sake of the other inmates of the field, should be removed and turned out alone. This may cause problems of its own, but the fact remains that 'innocent' horses must not be made to suffer because of one fly in the ointment. Kickers often kick humans, too, who are less able to retaliate than other horses.

Laminitis

Commonly called 'fever in the feet' or 'founder', this foot disorder is extremely painful for the horse and, if allowed to go unchecked it can become serious to the extent that the horse has to be destroyed. It is caused by disorders (usually overfeeding or toxins in the blood for some other reason) which cause an alteration in the blood flow to and within the feet. The outer, horny wall of the foot is joined to the inner, fleshy part covering the bones by vertical leaves of horn interlocking with fleshy, blood-containing leaves. This interlocking system holds the bones of the foot in place inside the wall.

In laminitis, the blood circulation is impaired, which starves the sensitive laminae of oxygen and nutrients, causing them to deteriorate and start separating from the horny laminae, breaking the bond between them. In bad cases the main bone of the foot, the pedal bone, starts to move, sometimes even piercing the horny and fleshy soles beneath it. The horny wall at the toe separates from the bone and the gap may fill with a degenerate, softer type of horn. This can be seen in the white line area at the toe as the line seems to widen and soften, often producing the condition known as seedy toe where cheesy-type horn exudes from the area.

In chronic cases, the foot may take on a concave appearance from the side, with a long toe and high heels. The toe wall may break away and produce a horizontal crack just below the coronet with the strain of walking on detached horn, while the heel horn continues to grow, giving the horse higher heels with upward slanting horn rings in the heel area.

Great strides have been made in the diagnosis and treatment of the different sorts of laminitis in recent years, mainly by the Laminitis Clinic at the University of Bristol in the UK. In bad cases, the detached wall at the toe is removed and supportive shoeing applied to prevent further movement of the pedal bone and to realign new horn growth in line with the new position of the pedal bone.

Apart from overfeeding and the circulation of toxins in the blood, or a chemical imbalance in the intestines due to faulty feeding, laminitis can be caused by concussion, but especially by incorrectly dressed (trimmed) feet. The overlong toe/low heels fashion of trimming, currently rather too common, not only in the UK, is a definite causative factor. It places inappropriate stresses on the sensitive tissues and can physically damage them. Feet must be dressed with the toes well back and the heels high enough to support the foot and leg.

Signs of laminitis are a pottering, short-stepped gait and a back-on-the-heels stance as the animal attempts to get his weight off the most painful part of the feet in the toe region. Usually both feet of a fore or hind pair are affected, but one foot, or all four, can be affected. If the animal lies down he often refuses to get up again because of the pain in his feet. If a foot is waved in the air, this indicates great pain.

If you suspect laminitis (and heat in the feet is not always present as the blood supply is reduced, not increased), muzzle your horse if he has to remain at grass, or bring him in on inedible bedding, and call the vet at once. If the animal is very lame, however, forcing him to walk can cause permanent and fatal damage, so leave him as he is. The vet should be called as an emergency and frog supports (maybe simply folded bandages taped to the feet) should be fitted. Corticosteroids should **NOT** be given as these will reduce the blood supply even further and do even more damage. They can even bring on laminitis when used in other diseases such as sweet itch.

Feel carefully with a finger all around the feet, immediately above the coronet. If you feel a 'ditch' or depression here this is a most serious sign as it indicates that the pedal bone is, indeed, moving, maybe at the front or maybe all round. However, provided the horse gets specialist help within 24 hours he may be saved. Many GP-type vets will prefer to refer the horse to a specialist in the treatment of laminitis.

Thrush

This is an infective foot ailment usually caused by dirty stables, ie horses standing on wet, dirty bedding, but I have also seen it in horses kept on wet land. The infection is assisted by the damp conditions and softened horn, and thrives, normally, in the inaccessible areas, such as by underrunning the frog. Horses affected by thrush usually go 'feeling' (cautiously) on the affected foot or feet because of the discomfort, may actually be lame (although as the lameness is often even in both feet, it can be difficult to spot) and 'paddle' (hop from foot to foot) when standing still.

Thrush smells foul and there is usually a dark discharge. If the frog is pressed with the hoofpick the horse will often show pain by flinching. Thrush is definitely a job for your veterinary surgeon as it will not clear up on its own. The horse will have to be brought in and the feet kept dry while the condition is treated.

Rings on the feet

Horn growth is greatly influenced by diet, and horses kept at grass, with its fluctuating growth pattern throughout the year, often develop 'grass rings' running horizontally round the feet. These are small ridges on the wall of the hoof and are quite normal in such cases, and nothing to worry about. In fact, they often appear in any horse, grass-kept or not, who has been subjected to a fairly sudden change of diet, ie one brought in after a season at grass.

Rings caused by laminitis are usually much more pronounced and, if the case has been a bad one, the hoof wall will often have 'sunk' in, giving a concave appearance to the foot when seen from the side. Once a horse has had laminitis it is always prone to another attack and these rings, caused by altered blood circulation to the feet which, in turn, affects the production of horn, should act as a warning to a potential purchaser or anyone put in charge of such a horse. (See also pages 90–2.)

6 Feeding and Watering

Feeding is the single most important subject to be mastered in horse management. A horse, like other animals, is what he eats. To the horse at grass, apart from disease or fatal injury, it is the one aspect of his care which can make the difference between life and death to him. Although, as we saw in the chapter on grassland management, his paddocks can, with care, be made to provide a good deal of his food, in winter or at times when he is working fairly hard, supplementary feeding will be needed. The type of food he can be given is just the same as for a stabled horse, although outdoor horses do not normally need roots and succulents such as carrots, apples, or soaked sugar beet pulp in their feeds as the grass provides the juicy element of their diet.

Digestive disorders seem to be much rarer in outdoor horses than in stabled ones, probably because their digestive systems are functioning more naturally, having a little food passing through them more or less constantly as in the wild. Even in winter, when the grass is practically useless from a nutritional point of view, horses still pick at it from instinct to keep that little something inside them all the time.

Their natural food, vegetation, is a fibrous food which takes up a lot of room in the intestine and which has to be consumed in large amounts to provide the horse with enough nutrients for his needs. This means the horse has to keep eating for about sixteen hours out of twenty-four just to take in his food requirement. Conversely, the food of meat-eating animals is very concentrated, and they can manage easily on one meal a day, or sometimes only one feast every few days. They need to spend little time eating, therefore, and their stomachs are comparatively large to accept the big, sudden intake, whereas the horse's stomach is small for his size because of his eating habits.

Purposes of food

Food is obviously needed to keep your horse alive, but its uses are given priority by his body. Food is used for:

1 Maintenance of body temperature at about 100.4°F (38°C).
2 Formation and replacement of body tissue (skin, muscle etc), bones, teeth, hair and horn.
3 Building up condition or putting on weight (storage of food reserves as fat).
4 Providing energy for life processes and movement. (Even standing still, your horse is using up energy to keep his heart beating, his lungs working and his digestion functioning.)

The first two requirements are the most important and if there is insufficient food and water to sustain them, the horse will die.

If a horse is worked hard and/or subjected to harsh weather on an inadequate ration, what nourishment there is will be used in priority to keep up body temperature (requiring more food or 'fuel' in cold weather), to replace tissue (more quickly used up during work) and to provide energy for these increased demands. On an inadequate ration, there is nothing left for body condition. In fact, the body releases some of its fat reserves to make up the deficit and the horse loses weight. If he exhausts these reserves of fat, he starts using his own body flesh (muscles, skin etc) to provide the fuel to keep up his temperature and just keep going using as little energy as possible, and eventually becomes emaciated. Vital tissues then suffer, body temperature drops – and the horse dies.

If the horse is not working and/or the weather is warm, yet the diet still inadequate, this process will still go on, but will take longer, as the food ration will not be used up so quickly.

Water
The body of the horse is about 70 per cent water and an ample supply is vital to life and health. Water is needed for

the body's fluids, such as blood, digestive juices, lymph and milk. It is also needed for the functioning of the excretory systems as the poisons produced by everyday living are excreted in urine, sweat, in vapour from the lungs and in droppings, which contain moisture. Water is, therefore, essential for the existence and working of the body and without an adequate supply the horse draws on his own body liquids to keep his system going. If he is worked hard in hot weather, he sweats profusely to help keep his temperature down. In either case, he can become dehydrated, so the production of body fluids becomes impossible, as does the maintenance of the body's systems, and death will result in a few days.

Constituents of food

The food constituents and their purposes are:
Carbohydrates (starches and sugar). Used for production of heat and energy. Excesses are stored around the body as fat for use when intake drops.
Proteins. These are the only foods which can make and repair body tissue, but can also supply some heat and energy. Some can be stored as fat, but then lose their tissue-building abilities, therefore a constant supply of protein in the diet is essential.
Fat. This is a good energy and heat producer and small amounts are needed for the absorption of the fat-soluble vitamins. Some researchers claim that up to 20 per cent of the entire diet for hard-working horses can be made up of fats (also called oils, lipids or lipins), as they are excellent concentrated sources of energy and are useful for feeding to high performance horses as a way of supplying extra energy without overloading them with concentrates. Horses with small appetites can also benefit from being fed a higher fat diet for the same reason.

The best way to feed extra oils is to give the horse soya, corn or maize oil in amounts recommended by a vet or nutritionist; possibly, as a guide, a tablespoon (15ml) per feed well mixed in. There is no need to follow the old practice of boiling linseed as the benefits of linseed can be provided more easily by using the products mentioned above. Also, linseed was (and still is in some quarters) used as a weekly or twice-weekly additive or as a linseed mash, going directly against one of the Golden Rules of feeding: to make no sudden changes. If you do want to feed boiled linseed you should feed a little in *every feed*, so that the horse's digestion is not upset by an erratic diet, for reasons given later. As this is impractical for most people, and linseed is unpalatable when kept in a fridge to prevent its going 'off' and fed cold, there is no point bothering with it.

Fibre (roughage). Needed to break up concentrated food (oats, barley, maize) for penetration by the digestive juices. Such food could otherwise impact into a doughy, impenetrable mass causing blockage, fermentation and possible rupturing of the intestine. Fibre also stimulates the movements of the intestine which push the food along and knead it up. Hay is a common and important source of fibre, also coarse grass and hayage products. Hayage is a moist substance which is simply grass conserved to a point midway between hay (a dry product) and silage (a grass product with a high moisture content). It is marketed to the horse world under various brand names. It is basically a roughage feed, but the higher energy grades can be used as a complete feed for horses in quite hard work. Horses should be gradually accustomed to it by introducing small amounts at first mixed with their hay, and gradually (over a period of two or three weeks or more) having the hayage portion of the ration increased and the hay portion decreased proportionately. The makers of hayage products advise that concentrates, if used, should be fed in smaller amounts with hayage than with hay, due to the higher feeding value of hayage.

Vitamins, minerals and trace elements. Needed in small quantities but nevertheless important. Foods possess differing amounts of these vital substances, which, in turn, have individual purposes. Modern farming methods often reduce the quantities of them in horses' food and a good comprehensive supplementary product is often an advantageous addition to the diet, fed in accordance with the directions on the package or upon specialist advice.

The main staple foods for horses (including cubes, or nuts and coarse mixes, which are an amalgam of different foods compounded together) contain different amounts of all these constituents. For example, although oats are mainly a carbohydrate food, they also contain protein (roughly 11 per cent to 14 per cent depending on the quality of the grain) and fibre in the form of the grain's husk, so no food fits solely into one category.

The horse's body can, when faced with a mildly unbalanced diet, convert some substances into others, and make some itself in its own intestines, so absolute precision in the formulation of a diet is not essential, and is, in any case, almost impossible when the horse has free access to grazing with the liberty to pick and choose which grasses he likes. To ensure a reasonably balanced diet, the land and grasses growing on it need assessing, and maybe analysing, by an expert nutritionist and the supplementary feeds formulating on top of that knowledge. If this sounds impractically ideal, it remains the most reliable way of working out a horse's full diet. Many owners, however, simply rely on assessing their horse's condition and providing supplementary feed (or not) in accordance with it. This does work to some extent, but the fact remains that the horse may be suffering from some slight deficiency, or in some cases a serious deficiency, of some essential nutrients. Excesses can also cause problems, so whether your horse is a family pet or a valuable broodmare or youngster, expert analysis and advice occasionally are well worth while.

Types of food

Basically, foods are divided into two main types for practical purposes – bulk, coarse or *roughage* foods such as hay, hayage, straw and chop (hay and/or straw chopped up small), and *concentrated* or energy foods such as grains (oats, barley, maize) and most compound feeds such as coarse mixes and cubes.

As discussed, all foods contain some elements of each

A horse in good, fit working condition, not so lean and 'tuned up' as a racehorse, but certainly not fat. An outdoor horse could carry more flesh in winter, for warmth

constituent (carbohydrate, protein etc), and it is the same with concentrates and roughage foods. Although hay is classed as a roughage or bulk food, containing much fibre, it also contains carbohydrates, proteins, a little fat and also vitamins, minerals and trace elements. Good hay, and particularly some of the hayage products now on the market, can alone provide an adequate balanced diet for light to moderate work.

How much, what and when?

A simple guide to working out how much food to give your horse is to take his height in hands and double it, reading the answer in pounds. For example, if your horse is 15 hands high, 15 x 2 = 30lb (13kg). I stress that this is a *rough guide* to use as a starting point, and represents the total poundage of all foods. For a stabled horse in medium work (two hours active hacking per day, riding-club-type work and so on), this should be split into one-third concentrates and two-thirds roughage.

Of course, a grass-kept horse is eating grass all the time so this confuses the issue except in winter when the grass is usually no good. Then, the above split would probably work well for a working horse living out in winter. The formula is on the slightly generous side, but a grass-kept horse must be fed to keep out the cold as well as provide for work.

A much more accurate way to determine a horse, cob or pony's dietary requirements as regards daily weight of food is to feed him according to his bodyweight, using the tables given here, or by taking him to a weighbridge if there is one within reasonable distance of your yard. Simply use a tape measure (or a piece of string, measured later) and pass it round your animal's girth just behind the wither. The result can be read off from the appropriate table, using the Ponies table for cobs. Of course, you have to know when your animal is too fat or too thin, and allow a little less or more as appropriate. Special measuring tapes are available from some feed firms and saddlers, or from the Equine Management Consultancy Service, 20 Victoria Road, Bulwark, Chepstow, Gwent, NP6 5QN, Wales.

Table 1. Ponies

Girth in inches	40	42.5	45	47.5	50	52.5	55	57.5
Girth in cm	101	108	114	120	127	133	140	146
Bodyweight in lb	100	172	235	296	368	430	502	562
Bodyweight in kg	45	77	104	132	164	192	234	252

Table 2. Horses

Girth in inches	55	57.5	60	62.5	65	67.5
Girth in cm	140	146	152	159	165	171
Bodyweight in lb	538	613	688	776	851	926
Bodyweight in kg	240	274	307	346	380	414

Girth in inches	70	72.5	75	77.5	80	82.5
Girth in cm	178	184	190	199	203	206
Bodyweight in lb	1014	1090	1165	1278	1328	1369
Bodyweight in kg	453	486	520	570	593	611

(Tables based on work of Glushanok, Rochlitz & Skay, 1981)

Once you know the bodyweight you can work out the total daily food requirement as, generally, horses will need 2kg of feed per 100kg of bodyweight (2lb/100lb) split as mentioned earlier. Ponies and cobs usually require less feed per lb or kg bodyweight than horses.

The tables show that just a ½in (1.23cm) change in girth can mean a 14-15lb (5-6kg) alteration in weight, which may not be noticeable to the eye. Also, take the measurement after the animal has just finished breathing out, or you could get a false reading.

Of course, grass-kept horses can be a real problem which is why expert advice on the state of your soil and grass should be taken so you can assess just how much nutrition your animal is getting from the grass and, therefore, what he might need in the way of supplementary feeding.

The old fetish about high-protein levels in feeds for hard-working horses is quite inappropriate: feeds should be assessed by *energy*, not protein, content, as even horses in full work do not need more than about 8 per cent protein in their total diet. Breeding stock (particularly growing youngsters), old horses and convalescents will need more.

For a riding-club-type horse out in winter, look for feeds which contain 10-12MJ (megajoules – a scientific unit of measurement) of digestible energy (DE) per kilogram. If the bag does not give such information contact the makers and ask for it, preferably in writing. For ponies, cobs and animals in light work, plus good doers, 8.5–10MJ of DE per kilogram is enough.

An eagle eye should be kept on the horse's bodyweight and condition at all times. A working horse should be in well covered but lean-ish condition: you should *not* be able to see his ribs, but you *should* be able to feel them fairly easily. With very fit endurance-type animals you could probably just see the last couple of pairs of ribs, which is acceptable provided the horse's top line is well muscled and he is not actually thin.

Assuming that the horse is in medium work most of the year, it can be taken that in winter he will need ad lib hay backed up by sufficient concentrates to maintain condition (bodyweight). In spring, summer and autumn, depending

An emaciated pony; note the angular shape, visible ribs and seemingly large head, exaggerated by the lack of flesh on the body

on the growth of grass, he will probably not need hay but could need concentrates for working energy. In spring, a problem could occur with protein-rich young grass causing overweight and laminitis and other digestive troubles, so supplementary feeding should not be given then. Much depends on the abundance and quality of the grazing available.

A horse which is much too fat, not only for work but for general good health; a prime candidate for laminitis

As a guide, if a grass-kept horse refuses hay, he is getting enough fibre and bulk from his grazing. Given normally good grazing, hay or hayage should be offered from about late September onwards and discontinued when the horses start leaving it in spring. Concentrates (which a grass-kept horse will rarely refuse even when rolling in fat) should be added mainly in winter or if grazing is poor and/or the horse working. Otherwise, good hay and grass are better feeds.

Eating creates heat as it uses energy and from a feeding point of view the best way to keep outdoor horses warm in winter is to make sure they have a constant supply of good hay or hayage which provides them with a natural central heating system. Carbohydrate (concentrate) feeds may provide more of an immediate boost of warmth-giving energy but their effects are relatively short-lived, and a hungry horse or one anxiously seeking out roughage or waiting for another short feed soon becomes cold, maybe dangerously so.

The horse digests his feed by means of enzymes and micro-organisms in the intestinal tract which live off his food and process it for him. Without an adequate healthy population of gut micro-organisms the horse could suffer chronic indigestion or colic and be unthrifty, with other digestive disorders. The micro-organisms are short-lived and need regular supplies of their different foods, different 'bugs' being responsible for digesting different foods. If the supply fails they die off, not only reducing their population and, therefore, the efficiency of the horse's digestive system, but also rotting down and causing a putrid environment in the gut which again can cause mild or serious colics. This is why it is important to give your horse the *same ingredients* in every feed and not to chop and change by giving, say, cubes for breakfast, coarse mix for lunch, barley for tea and so on. Alter the amounts of your ingredients if appropriate, but include at least a little of everything normally fed in each feed.

It is also a bad practice to feed a mash (usually the familiar, old bran mash) once or twice a week. Bran is not a good horse food. It contains too much phosphorous and far

too little calcium, and this imbalance can create bone problems, even if barely noticeable, but which could be responsible for such things as the horse easily becoming concussed
on hard going, throwing splints or going frequently but inex-
plicably 'feeling' or actually lame. Bran (or other) mashes
constitute a complete and sudden change in feeding which is
very bad for the horse's digestive system. Bran mashes are
not easy to digest; on the contrary, they irritate the horse's
digestive tract and this is why they appear to have a laxative
effect as that system tries to get rid of the offending material
as quickly as possible. This is *not* good feeding policy, obviously, and the practice of mashing horses is not now recommended by nutritionists and many up-to-date vets.

If you want to give your horse a low-energy feed (he
should not need an actual laxative if his feeding is correct)
because of reduced work, give chop (maybe the molassed
kind) with soaked sugar beet pulp and, if you wish, grass
meal and/or some other roots such as carrots or apples (plus
one handful of his usual concentrate) and make sure these
ingredients, even in small amounts, are present in his other
feeds. This way you will keep his digestive bugs alive and
thriving and your horse comfortable and correctly, *consis-
tently* fed as he would be in nature.

Horses needing most feeding, of any type, are those in
hard work, breeding stock and elderly animals. If in doubt as
to your horse's diet, do consult a vet or an equine nutritionist
or management consultant.

The horse's condition as a guide

Keeping a careful eye on your horse's condition or bodyweight is a good practical way of assessing his food requirements. You must first know your horse well when in normal
condition for the work you want him to do. Is he naturally a
rounded, chunky type, or the lean, more angular sort? When
you are familiar with the 'real him' you will know whether
his outdoor life is causing him to become too fat or too thin,
and can act accordingly.

Even when resting, a horse should not be allowed to grow

too fat because of the risk of tendon strain and laminitis. Conversely, if he is too thin, he will have a lowered resistance to disease and the ravages of the weather and flies.

Apart from his general appearance, the parts of a horse which most quickly show condition are his top line (upper neck, back, loins and quarters) and his belly. In summer, assessment is easy, but it is more difficult when hampered by a thick and maybe long winter coat. In winter, therefore, get into the habit of really digging your fingers through his coat and feeling how much flesh he has on him over his top line area. You should not be too aware of his ribs and hips but rather have to feel and press for them.

Bearing in mind his individual make and shape, then, generally a thin horse will show a lack of flesh or muscular development along the top of his neck. A giveaway sign is if the neck appears to sink in front of the withers. His withers and spine will be noticeable to both look and feel, his so-called hip bones (in fact, they are the pelvic bones) will be prominent (often known as hat-racks!), and his quarters will show a lack of flesh by appearing to 'fall away' or sink away from his hips and croup, and maybe even showing 'poverty lines' from front to back and down the backs of the thighs when seen from behind. His belly, instead of being rounded and seeming to continue all the way to his stifles (at the tops of his hind legs) will probably show an upward-running line from front to back underneath, and the horse will look pinched in (known as 'tucked up') in the area between belly and hind legs.

A fat horse often takes on a barrel-like appearance and a waddle to go with it. He could develop a big, 'bull' neck, hefty shoulders and huge pads of fat on both sides of his spine. His belly will be gross and low-slung while his quarters will look 'appley' and rounded with fat. He will actually feel soft if you prod him, rather than sleek and hard as a fit horse. Between these two extremes of the slab-sided, starved horse and the walking barrel is the ideal for your horse. Only you can really get to know him and assess his condition and fitness (about which more in Chapter 8) to ensure he is just right.

Practical considerations

The entire object of feeding your horse is to make sure he gets his ration down him one way or another. This he will not do if it is just tipped on to the ground to be trampled in winter mud, blown away or stolen by other horses. It is always more economical to give both hay and concentrates in some sort of container.

A popular way of giving hay is to fill a haynet and tie it up in the shed (there should be at least one more net than there are horses so that the timid ones always have one to go to) or to tie it to a fence post and top rail for firm support. Nets sag lower as they empty and hooves can easily become entangled in them, so they should be tied at horse's head height when possible. They can also be tied to a convenient tree branch against the trunk. If all else fails, hay can be fed in a mobile field rack often seen for cattle, the rack being moved daily to prevent poaching the land. It is always best to feed hay under cover in the shed to prevent its being spoiled by rain. Again, nets can be used, or a long rack can be fixed along the back wall at horse's head height.

Concentrates can be fed in wide shallow cattle buckets or even plastic washing-up bowls if the horses are quiet eaters who will not tip up the container and spill the contents. The containers can be put on the ground at least 16ft (5m) apart, which is outside the horse's natural 'personal distance', and here it is best for at least one person to stay around to see fair play, and that each gets his proper ration. Quiet, friendly horses can have their containers on the floor of the shed. Do not leave buckets or bowls around after the horses have finished as they can be a source of injury.

Horses who waste their feed by throwing it around can be fed from portable travel mangers which hook on to the fence or on to a strong bar on the wall of the shed. These mangers may have two bars running from front to back of them across the top to prevent a horse scooping food out with his nose.

Any animal who is timid and constantly chivvied by the others may not be able to eat his concentrates in peace, so should be brought out of the field for the twenty minutes or so it will take him to eat up.

A word about feeding cubes alone to grass-kept horses. Although rare, it has been known for cases of ruptured stomach to occur when the easily chewed up cubes meet up with the soft soggy grass in the stomach, forming a stiff, gooey mass of food which is hard for the digestive juices to penetrate. It is always safer to mix a double handful of chop (also known as chaff) with the cubes to ensure the presence of sufficient fibrous roughage to break up the food. If the horse winkles out the cubes from the chop, use molassed chaff, which most horses like. Bran is is less good for this than chop, and not advisable in large amounts.

Horses should not be given more than about 4lb (1.8kg) total feed of concentrates at one time. The stomach works best when two-thirds full, and if more food then keeps coming in, food which is not yet adequately digested by the stomach muscles and digestive juices could be released further down into the intestine to make room for the continuing input, and cause colic. This means that if your horse is needing 8lb (3.6kg) concentrates a day he will have to have two feeds, necessitating two visits to the field, say morning and night. If he needs more than this, at least three visits are going to be needed. Two visits a day should be paid anyway but you can possibly cut out the third visit by feeding very good hay with a high feeding value, so you will not need to supplement with so many concentrates. If good hay is unavailable, use one of the hayage products. These are available in different protein and energy levels and can often drastically reduce the amount of other foods needed. Consult your vet about this, if required. However, remembering what has been explained about the workings of the digestive system and the micro-organisms, efforts should be made to give two feeds of concentrates, if very small, as this makes for better digestion and less risk of problems.

Most people stress that horses should be fed at regular times, otherwise they gather around the gates, become impatient and fractious and start scrapping with each other. In practice, I find that an owner need not tie himself or herself to rigid times *provided* the horses are never allowed to get really hungry, which they will not when grass is plentiful or, when it is not, they have enough hay left with them to last them easily until the next feed time. Half an hour to an hour late now and then will not be the end of the world in such circumstances. Do not, however, miss a feed completely, and do not feed on some days and not on others, even if the horses' workloads are erratic. Once you start supplementary feeding, keep it up, but adjust the ration by quantity, if necessary. Routine *is* important to the horse. If animals are to receive only one concentrate feed a day, make it at night, so that they have the benefit of 'central heating' for the colder hours of the night.

Storage can be a problem in the case of isolated fields, unless you have adequate transport to take the full rations needed on each visit, ready packed in haynets and buckets. If you are using a barn as a shelter, perhaps part of it could be securely partitioned off for feed storage, preferably locked, or a building could be rented at a nearby farm. Remember you will also need storage for other equipment, even if you carry your tack or harness each day. It is preferable to be able to store veterinary supplies and grooming kit nearby, and New Zealand rugs, rather than be forced to transport your horse's entire life-support system every time you visit him.

Water sources have already been mentioned in Chapter 3, together with the fact that a horse can need up to 12 gallons (551) of water a day when working hard or in hot weather. Whether the water is from a natural source such as a stream or pond (regularly checked for pollution) or from a trough or plastic dustbins, the supply must be checked at least once a day (bins need filling to the top twice daily, depending on number, as a horse may be reluctant to put his head down to the bottom for a drink), access to the source must be kept secure and inviting (no rough going such as rubble, and with mud lessened by scattering used bedding thickly on badly poached areas, as described earlier) and time should be taken now and then to watch and see if any animal is being persistently chased away from water. If so, he should be watered separately morning and night before being given his feed. He will be quite all right on this method *provided he is allowed to drink his fill at each watering.* He will drink, then probably lift his head and look around, resting. In all likelihood, he will then drop his head for another drink, but it is always better to let him leave the water source himself rather than be led away. Then you can be sure he really has had enough.

Although good modern stable (and field) management indicates that water should always be available (and I agree with this) the fact remains that this is not so in the wild. Herds of animals often make long treks to water holes morning and night, returning to their grazing grounds in between. They do not hang around the water all day, so if a horse in your care needs separate watering do not worry about him. He will be quite all right watered ad lib, night and morning. Do water him first and feed him (if necessary) afterwards. He will doubtless have some grass in his stomach, but concentrates can cause problems if given before a full draught of water. Water intake can be increased by feeding salt to an animal, and many people forget to provide a salt lick for horses at grass. It is advisable to place a salt lick on the wall of the shelter in a plastic (not metal) holder, but do not site it over a water container.

7 Turn-out and Clothing

Structure and function of skin and coat

The only things separating your horse from the rigours of the environment are his skin and coat; and the thickness of the skin varies from only 4mm (⅕in) down to less than 1mm (¹⁄₂₅in) (depending on its location on the body and the breed of horse).

The skin has two main layers, an inner layer called the dermis and an outer layer called the epidermis. It is the dermis which contains the hair follicles, the sebaceous glands which secrete oil (sebum) to lubricate and waterproof skin and hair and which open into the hair follicles, and also the sweat glands which excrete sweat on to the skin to help to get rid of waste products and to cool down the body by carrying some excess heat to the surface for evaporation. It contains nerve endings and blood vessels; it also contains the means of manufacturing vitamin D.

The epidermis is composed of dead, horny cells which protect the dermis. These cells are gradually shed (being replaced by cells from the dermis below) and are seen as the dandruff in an ungroomed horse's coat. The epidermis also contains the colouring pigment, melanin, which strengthens and helps protect the skin. White markings usually have pink skin underneath, which really means the skin (which obtains its pinkness from the blood) is colourless, in fact, and so without the added protection of melanin. This is why white legs and the large white patches on coloured horses (known as piebalds and skewbalds in Britain and pintos or paints in the USA) are often more susceptible to the weakening effects of weather and so more prone to conditions like mud fever and allergies.

Skin protects the body from germs, foreign bodies,

sunlight and poisonous substances, it provides the horse with his sense of touch, enabling him to tell the difference between hot and cold, pain and pleasure, friction, pressure and relief. The hair which grows from the skin assists in some of its functions, giving added protection against weather and temperature. The mane and tail hair also protect the horse against the outside world, and the tail in particular is useful for helping dislodge flies from the back half of the body.

Skin is thicker over the areas most exposed to weather and prone to injury, such as the top part of the neck, shoulders, back, loins and quarters and also the fronts and outer sides of the legs, being thinner in the other, more sheltered areas. Growth of coat hair coincides with this pattern, being thinner on the lower part of the body and inside the legs, and also around sensory areas such as muzzle (the horse's equivalent to fingers) and eyes.

The coat has two main forms, the short summer coat and the longer winter coat. The thickness or thinness of the coat is related to the length of the hairs and not to their number, longer hairs obviously overlapping more and so making the coat appear 'thick', and vice versa. Nature has 'programmed' the horse to shed, in stages, his thick winter coat in spring, when the climate warms up and the days lengthen, and to similarly cast his short summer coat in autumn and replace it with longer hairs for the colder winter months.

Grooming and shampooing

Generally, the rules of good horse management discourage owners from body brushing and shampooing grass-kept horses as these procedures remove natural grease from skin and coat and, therefore, much of the horse's protection. It is possible to produce a clean-looking horse without heavy body brushing or shampooing, although your horse will never be as clean as a stabled animal. Light body brushing will do enough to make the horse presentable without stripping him of too much coat grease, even through a winter coat. Remove dust and dried mud from the coat either with a dandy brush (and possibly a plastic or rubber curry) in the normal way, or with a vacuum groomer used lightly. These are useful especially for a mudcaked, wintercoated teddy bear of a horse. Follow up by a light body brushing and a final wipe over with a damp stable rubber. The mane and tail can be washed as normal, when necessary.

It is best not to shampoo a grass-kept horse, especially in winter, unless he is going somewhere really special, as this will obviously remove nearly all his natural oils, and they will not be replaced in time for his return to the field. You can get away with it occasionally if you have a waterproof rug to put on the horse for a day or two afterwards (even if he does not normally wear one) but generally it should be avoided. If done, the horse must be dried very quickly and thoroughly.

The horse should, on a daily basis, have his eyes, nostrils and lips damp-sponged clean of dried-on discharges (not only for cleanliness but to help avoid chapping in winter and fly-strike in summer), and the whole under-tail area cleaned, too, with a different sponge. The inside of the sheath of geldings and stallions should not be just damp-sponged, which has little effect on the greasy discharge (smegma) in this area, but washed every two weeks or so with warm water and a mildly medicated soap on the 'back end' sponge. Rinse with the sponge very thoroughly (adding a dash of mild antiseptic to the water) and smear inside the sheath with a little liquid paraffin which helps prevent the smegma sticking to the skin. It is also excellent for rubbing into the entire lower leg area of horses susceptible to mud fever as a protection, as is udder cream or E45 barrier cream (available from most good chemists). These will all have to be washed off occasionally with mild, medicated soap and renewed.

Feet should be picked out daily and checked not only for the fit (and presence) of shoes but for softening horn in wet weather or cracks if the ground is hard. Particularly in winter, even if the legs are caked with mud, put your hands on the heel, pastern and fetlock area for several seconds to feel if there is any abnormal heat which could herald the onset of mud fever.

It pays to tease out and gently brush the mane and tail daily, to help prevent a build-up of tangles which are time-consuming to remove and almost certain to cause broken hairs in the process.

If the horse is being prepared for a special day, it makes your task easier to bring him in to a cool, well-ventilated stable the night before. It will be almost impossible to get him respectably clean on the morning of the event if he has been out all night (especially in winter). One night indoors will not soften him up and he should spend the next night out as normal.

Trimming

Even though your horse does live out, there is no need for him to look unkempt with a rough, overlong mane and tail. Mane and forelock can be pulled to thin them out, if necessary for manageable plaits, and shortened to a length of about 5 or 6in (12-15cm) (depending on the size of the horse) by just snapping off the ends of the hairs with the fingertips in a quick, snatching movement. If your horse objects to pulling, a razor comb (from many chain stores) used underneath from the roots has just as good an effect and does not produce a bristly re-growth.

The tail of a grass-kept horse should not be pulled at the top but left full. Racehorses have, in many cases, full tails at the top combined with a neat, level 'bang' at the bottom, and look lovely. To bang a tail, get a friend to stand with an arm under the dock so that the tail falls as it does when the horse is in action. Get hold of all the hairs inside your fist at the bottom of the dock, run your hand down to just below hock level, and cut off the hairs below this evenly with sharp, large scissors.

The tail should not be longer than this in winter or it will get clogged with mud and snow, although in summer it can be left a little longer to help with the fly problem. The top of the tail can be plaited for special occasions if the hair is too thick to look elegant left full. Do not be tempted to pull it; horses stand with their tails to wind and rain in winter and

A full (unpulled) banged tail, sometimes known as a 'racehorse' tail. Grass-kept animals should retain the hair on the dock for protection against bad weather. This type of tail can easily be plaited up for special occasions, and could be banged to a slightly shorter length in winter to avoid clogging with mud and snow

the dock hairs spread out and protect the sensitive areas between the buttocks, so helping prevent heat loss. Standing this way, with the full protection of his natural tail and the thicker skin on back and quarters, the horse presents a small body area to the elements and is able to protect his all-important head and the underparts of his body from the weather. (In summer, horses often stand broadside to the sun, to absorb maximum sunlight and warmth – the opposite to their winter stance.)

Long hairs under the jaw can be trimmed off (with fingers or scissors) without much detriment, although they do act as drainage hairs in wet weather. Opinions vary as regards fetlock hair. Some claim it is best to leave most of it, at least on the point of the fetlock, again for drainage, while others maintain legs are easier to keep clean, and to treat if mud fever develops, if excess hair is removed. I tend to find that if a horse is susceptible to mud fever, he will get it, hair or no hair, and feel it best to compromise by removing the shaggiest growth but leaving enough on the point of the fetlock to help drain away water.

Trimming off the long whiskers from muzzle and eyes is another bone of contention. These whiskers are the horse's feeler hairs and some animals become most disorientated, refusing to eat and banging their heads, if they are clipped off (they should *never* be pulled out). Others do not seem to bother. Personally, I prefer to leave them on.

Clipping

Whether you clip at all or not depends on the work you will be giving your horse and the weight of winter coat he grows. If the horse is a breedy type with a short coat and you are not doing any very active work in winter, such as hunting, you could well manage without clipping, but if you want to work him fairly hard and/or his coat is very woolly, some of it will have to come off if the horse is not to sweat heavily and get chilled and probably lose condition.

A normal trace clip, the most extensive clip which should be given to a grass-kept horse in winter. Trace-clipped animals can be made quite fit enough to hunt respectably, even in galloping country, or to undertake extended hacks or drives. They do need a proper shelter shed, and almost certainly a New Zealand or other waterproof rug

Provided he is hardy enough, a horse living out without a rug or temporarily without a shed can have the hair on his breast and under his neck clipped if in work. The hair should be left everywhere else, to provide some protection from the weather and mud

An 'Irish' clip, where the hair is removed as in a trace clip, but the line is tapered off at the stifle, leaving the hair on the thighs. The belly hair could be left on up to the dotted line, for further protection. This is a good clip for a horse in light to moderate work

Having stressed the necessity for a proper field shed in an earlier chapter, I am assuming that there is one, kept well bedded down, and in such circumstances, with the addition of a waterproof rug, the horse can be given a trace clip with no harm resulting.

A trace clip removes the hair from under the neck, breast, belly and round the tops of the legs, as shown in the illustration. Even so, I think it best to clip once only in early to mid autumn so that a little hair will re-grow, and to leave it at that. Remember, even moving about their field horses kick up a certain amount of mud on to their bellies and without the protection of hair there, chapped skin and mud fever can so easily occur. If the horse is having to manage without a shed (for a short period while arrangements to provide one are in progress), he will lie down (if at all) on wet, muddy ground. If he is even trace clipped, he will have little or nothing to protect his underparts from the mud and, again, could suffer from skin complaints. In such cases, the hair can be removed from the breast and under the neck as shown. I should feel it wrong to clip more extensively than this until a bedded-down shelter were available.

Many people feel a head looks smarter clipped in winter and no doubt it does, but with a grass-kept horse it should not be done. The ears can be tidied up by holding their edges together and carefully cutting off with scissors any hair protruding beyond them, particularly at the base, but that is all. If this is done, and the long under-jaw hairs neatened up, he will not look too bad at all.

Waterproof clothing and headcollars

There are as many differing views on the advantages and disadvantages of waterproof rugs as there are on most other aspects of equestrianism and horse management. Some maintain these rugs are more trouble than they are worth and cause problems of their own (which they can) and others say they are an absolute boon and they could never survive the winter (on behalf of their horse) without one (which may well be true). My view is that *properly fitted and maintained* water-

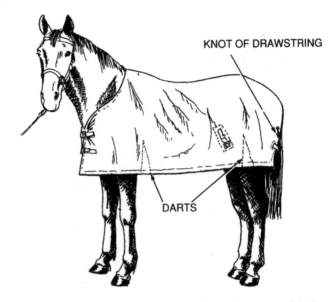

KNOT OF DRAWSTRING

DARTS

A well-fitting New Zealand pattern waterproof rug. It comes well in front of the withers and extends beyond the root of the tail; it is shaped to fit the horse's spine; there are two breast buckles (the top one can be fitted more loosely than the bottom one, to allow the horse to graze in comfort); it has no surcingle (which hinders the circulation of air, and prevents the rug from returning to position after rolling or lying down), and is shaped at the elbows and stifle. It has hindleg straps, and the drawstring inside the hem over the root of the tail can be pulled close to ensure a 'personalised' fit against the weather

proof rugs can definitely be a considerable comfort to a fine-coated or clipped horse living out in winter.

There are three main types available, although many saddlers produce their own designs. The best type, in my experience, is the original pattern from New Zealand which gives waterproof rugs the name by which they are all known in Britain, whether they are the true New Zealand design or not.

This pattern is shaped along the back (spine) seam to conform to the shape of the horse. It has large shaping darts at elbow and stifle to take up the slack fabric (normally canvas or tough sailcloth), breast straps across the front, leg straps at the back, a drawstring fitted inside the turning on the back edge over the root of tail/buttocks area which can be pulled to achieve an individual fit, and, most importantly, it has *no* surcingle. Because of the shaping and the freedom

An Australian pattern waterproof rug, with frontleg straps and a fillet strap round the thighs. This rug is properly shaped and does not need a surcingle

enabled through the lack of surcingle, horses can buck, gallop, play about, lie down and roll, get up and shake and the rug will return to its correct position. Air can circulate freely under the rug (helping to ensure healthy skin) while the horse remains warm and dry.

The second best type of rug (again in my experience) is the Australian pattern. This is also shaped but has frontleg straps, not back (see above), a fillet strap behind the thighs to stop the back end blowing up in the wind, and, again, no surcingle. These rugs are quite good but do not stay in place quite as well as the New Zealand pattern.

The third and most common type is often insufficiently shaped, if at all, has breast and hindleg straps and a surcingle. The surcingle, far from keeping the rug in place, actually prevents the rug's returning to its correct position after the horse has lain down and/or rolled. The rug moves under the surcingle, which then prevents it moving back again. The surcingle not only inhibits the free circulation of air under the rug but also causes pressure on the spine (a heinous crime in horse management) and so a potentially, or actually, sore back – and a horse with a sore back, whether a ride or drive horse, is out of commission. If you already have a waterproof rug which is properly shaped and has a surcingle, provided it is a good fit and you adjust the breast and leg straps properly, you should be able to remove the surcingle and, so, its associated disadvantages, and still find the rug stays in place quite well.

Some rugs are made of heavy sailcloth or canvas and are half lined with wool for warmth, others are of synthetic fabrics with various linings or filling material. Straps are either of leather or strong synthetic material. Whichever type you buy, never consider any rug which is not properly shaped along the back seam, at elbows and stifle and over the tail, and do not buy a rug with a surcingle.

If you already own a poorly shaped rug with a surcingle and cannot afford to replace it, it can be greatly improved by sewing inside it, to the lining and taking care not to pierce the outer covering, four pieces of thick, old-fashioned numnah felt (obtainable from similarly good old-fashioned saddlers) on either side of the back seam where the highest point of the withers goes, and also on either side at the back area directly under the surcingle (see page 121). The felt should be at least an inch (2cm) thick, and will raise the rug off withers and spine and 'wedge' the rug in place, vastly improving the rug's effectiveness and the horse's comfort. (A saddler would probably add elbow and stifle darts for you, in which case you could probably remove the surcingle.)

Fit

Waterproof rugs should be slightly roomier than stable rugs. They must come well in *front* of the withers round the base of the neck, not with the neckline resting on top of the withers or on the shoulders. At the back, they should extend a few inches beyond the root of the tail. Depth-wise, they should come a hand's breadth below the elbow and stifle. The breast straps must be fastened so that they keep the front end where it belongs but allow you to pass the flat of your hand comfortably over the withers under the rug and permit the horse to get his head down to graze without

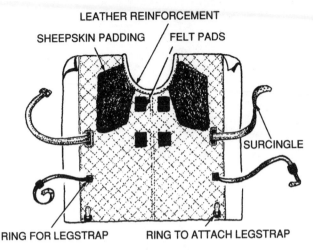

If your rug has a surcingle, you can improve its comfort and security by sewing thick felt pads to the lining. Those at the withers lift the rug off the horse, and those a little further back prevent the surcingle pressing on to the spine. The pads 'wedge' the rug in position on either side of the spine and help stop it slipping and the sheepskin padding at the shoulders minimises rubbing

significant pressure where his neck joins his breast. He will have his head down most of the time, remember, and tightness here can eventually cause sufficient discomfort to prevent his grazing freely and pull the rug to cause pressure on the withers.

Even in well shaped rugs with no surcingle, improvement can be made and wither pressure eliminated by adding felt pads inside at the withers. Sheepskin padding here simply lessens friction; it cannot remove pressure. Some fine-coated horses also need sheepskin padding at the shoulders to prevent excessive wearing away of hair (the first stages of friction sores). Synthetic fleece is usually too harsh for such horses and does not solve the problem.

There are two leg straps at the back in New Zealand and similar pattern rugs, with a variety of simple fastenings and length adjustments. One end of each strap will fasten about a third of the way forward from the back edge and there will be another fastening, usually a 'D' ring, on or just inside the back edge.

The best way to fasten the leg straps so that they keep the

This method of fastening the hindleg straps (linking one through the other) helps prevent the straps rubbing the thin skin inside the gaskins, as the straps hold each other away from the legs

This poor horse is in a great deal of discomfort. The headcollar is much too large, and could easily be rubbed or pulled off; it is sliding down his neck, and pulling on his nose. The rug comes too far up underneath the neck, but is too far back on the withers, where it is pulling, and will eventually cause soreness. It is not properly shaped at the elbows and stifle, and the surcingle exerts pressure on the spine. The leg straps are a little too long for safety, and should only just be visible

rug in place and do not rub the sensitive skin inside the horse's hind legs is as follows: take the left strap at its forward fastening and, making sure it is not twisted, pass it out between the horse's hind legs at the back and clip it to its fastening on the left of the back edge. Now take the right strap and again pass it out between the horse's hind legs, *linking it through the left strap,* then clipping it to its ring on the right of the back edge of the rug. Each strap is now fastened at both ends on its own side of the rug and round the appropriate hind leg, but the straps hold each other away from the inside of the legs and help prevent chafing.

Some rugs hang better if the straps are criss-crossed between the legs, so that the left strap clips to the right back edge and vice versa. Trial and error will decide the best method for your horse and rugs, but try the first method to start with as this is nearly always the most satisfactory.

When the leg straps are fastened, adjust their length so that you can only *just* see them level with the bottom edge of the rug. Adjusted like this, it is extremely unlikely that the horse will tread on them or get both legs 'down one hole'. If they are too short they will annoy him, rub and restrict his movements; if too long, he might tread on them, entangle his legs and have a nasty accident.

Maintenance

Rugs should be removed twice daily, the horse thoroughly inspected for signs of rubbing (rubbed or worn hair, sore or even raw skin) and the rug changed, or replaced if not too wet. You will need two rugs to enable you to remove excess mud and dry off one rug while the other is in use. If the rug is an extra-depth one it will cover the correctly adjusted leg straps, obviously.

Once your horse starts wearing a rug you will have to keep it on until spring as he will become used to it. If you leave the rug off during a mild day and the horse gets wet, he will have to be thoroughly dried before wearing the rug again or dampness under the rug will probably cause skin problems, unless the rug is one of the permeable ones.

Periodically during the winter, if weather permits, and

certainly at the end of each winter, the rugs should be laundered and repaired, and reproofed with a suitable product from a tack or camping shop before being put away for the summer. Synthetic rugs can normally be laundered in a washing machine but canvas and sailcloth ones cannot. Vacuum their linings thoroughly before scrubbing them with warm soapy water and thoroughly hosing out the soap. Hose and scrub off mud from the outside and spread over a fence or hedge to dry completely before reproofing the outside and having any repairs done. Leather parts must be kept cleaned and well oiled throughout the winter and metal parts should be lightly smeared with oil.

Accustoming a horse to a New Zealand rug

Most horses take kindly to their 'macs' but some dislike the feel of leg straps in strange places, so must be gradually accustomed to them.

Put the rug on first in the stable, having let the horse sniff it well. Adjust the straps correctly and lead the horse round his box, in a bridle for extra control. As soon as he is calm in it, lead him round the stable yard, and ultimately lunge him in the rug. Make sure he is quite unworried in it, even if it takes a few days, before turning him loose in the field, as although he is unlikely to suffer harm from the rug itself if correctly fitted, he might gallop in a panic and hurt himself in other ways.

Ancillary clothing

Head and neck hoods are also available for outdoor wear, although not commonly seen. The types made from stretch fabric and fitting closely are uncomfortable for the horse. Neck and head hoods normally attach to each other, with the neck hood remaining open under the gullet, apart from retaining straps, and fastening (overlapping) to the front part of the rug. Obviously the rug must have attachments for the hood and it is usually necessary to buy integrated clothing from one manufacturer. These extra items of clothing can certainly be useful in very cold, wet weather and/or for sensitive horses.

A good type of headcollar; the browband permits a fly-fringe to be fitted in summer, and prevents the headpiece from slipping down the neck and causing an uncomfortable pull on the nose. There is ample room around the ears, and the horse has space to move his jaws when eating. The buckles allow precise adjustment of fit; the noseband does not rub the cheekbones, but cannot be rubbed off

Headcollars

It is best to turn out a horse without a headcollar unless he is hard to catch because there is always the chance of his catching it on any projection, such as a branch in the hedge.

Do use a browband on your headcollar as this makes for greater comfort and security. It prevents the headpiece sliding down the neck and causing an uncomfortable pull on the front of the noseband. The headpiece and browband should fit comfortably around the base of the ears allowing room to pass a finger easily around the area and so that neither strap cuts in. The noseband should fall midway between the sharp face bone and the corner of the mouth and you should be able to fit no more than four fingers inside the noseband. Headcollars with adjusting buckles on the noseband are recommended.

You will not wish to turn out your horse in your best leather headcollar. Chrome tanned leather (as opposed to vegetable tanned), which is often pale green, is a useful compromise for field use. It stretches more before breaking, and New Zealand (and other) rug leg straps are often made of it. Although the headcollar will become regularly muddy, still take the time to clean and oil it often during use to keep it soft. Smear metal parts lightly with oil.

Nylon webbing headcollars, and some other synthetic materials, are extremely strong and so can be dangerous if left on turned-out horses, as they will not snap at all easily if caught up.

8 Working and Resting

Working a horse off grass, even quite hard, is not as impossible as many people think it is. It is true a grass-kept horse cannot be made as supremely fit as, say, a racehorse or three-day-event horse where fast work is performed by an animal carrying no excess fat (a condition difficult to achieve in a horse with constant access to grass), but there are many endurance horses (whose work is slower although very demanding) who perform very successfully while spending a considerable amount of time at grass.

The main 'secret' is that your grass should be of poorish to medium quality compared with normal farming standards. This should not be too difficult to manage if you have taken expert grassland advice as suggested in Chapter 4, or, if unable to sow your own land, have chosen rented grazing carefully (briefly, land supporting sheep will probably be suitable, that carrying dairy cattle will not). Your horse's nutritional requirements can then be made up with 'hard' feed (concentrates) which help promote hard condition for strenuous work. If the grazing is really poor, he will need hay, too, so his diet will approximate even more to that of a stabled horse, and your task will be that much easier.

Poor quality grazing must not, however, be confused with scrub, neglected land bearing many weeds or poisonous plants; it is simply land which has been sown with grasses having a moderate nutritional content. It should still be well cared for and kept clean and in good heart. It could also be land grazed down by beef cattle, or in areas where the soil is not of the best.

In addition, it is an aid to physical fitness if the field is large and undulating as the horse has further to roam and the differing gradients assist in muscular development.

Getting fit

The fittening process for a grass-kept horse is, in principle, exactly the same as for a stabled one – a gradual increase of work and exercise. The main differences are that with the grass-kept animal you do not begin grooming with the body brush, at least not hard, because even in summer some grease and dandruff give added resistance to the skin and coat. Feeding may cause a quandary because of the grass. In winter, feed as for a stabled horse. In spring, watch the grass and the horse's condition very carefully. If the grass is at all rich and lush and the horse is putting on weight but you cannot bring him in, either move him to a poorer field (easier said than done, maybe) or cut out all his other food and give him long walks on the roads or bridlepaths. If he has been out all winter and/or in regular work anyway, two hours walking a day will do him nothing but good, plus, perhaps, a little slow trotting.

Once the spring flush is over the grass is less rich and lush and you can start fittening work in earnest, judging by your own circumstances whether the horse needs concentrates or not. Make him walk up to his bridle, and trot, too, but steadily. Once a fair degree of fitness has been reached (after, say, a month's walking and trotting) you can, in fact, give the horse more trotting than you would with a stabled horse because he will be walking about the field all day anyway, albeit not marching on in the way he would be asked to do when ridden, so will do much of the slow work for you. However, unless the ground gets hard in summer, his legs will not be hardened without road work to make demands on them, so steady (working pace) trotting on the roads is still part of his programme.

Once the stage of cantering under saddle is reached, the horse may well be as fit as when stabled provided the grass is not too rich or plentiful. You will know your own horse and will be able to compare him in the two states – stabled and grass-kept – but you may well be pleasantly surprised to find that he does not develop a grass belly, that he does not puff and sweat as much as you thought he would and that he really is fitter than you thought you could get him. The three main points to remember are:

1 Avoid rich, lush grass in spring and summer and give plenty of walking and steady trotting at these times to keep him 'tuned up'.
2 It is not necessary for a horse to be body brushed hard to get him fit. The rain will remove excess dandruff anyway and his skin will be perfectly healthy functioning in natural conditions.
3 His lungs will probably be all the better for his outdoor life (indeed, it may have been a respiratory disorder which brought on your decision to keep him out in the first place) and will serve his heart and circulatory system, and so the rest of his body, even better than when stabled – a considerable bonus.

Grass-kept working horses are easier to keep fit than stabled ones as they do not go 'stale' in their work or develop cornsickness (which is mild indigestion due to an unrelieved high concentrate diet). They will stay fit and happy longer provided their normal requirements of food, company and shelter are constantly taken care of. They do not get bored (half the problem with a stabled animal) or develop vices. To keep your horse fit, simply pay close attention to his physical condition, slacken off the work slightly once the desired level of fitness has been achieved and, again, avoid over-rich grazing. As with a stabled animal, vary his work and keep him interested and active, and you should be rewarded with a horse almost constantly fit for your needs. Many horses kept out are likely to be required for work all year round, but remember that the harder they work the more likely they are to need a break (as with a stabled horse). The type of horse kept out like this, though, will probably be doing riding-club or local show or event work during warm times of year and, perhaps, cub-hunting and/or hunting proper at other times, and will probably never need a prolonged break from work.

Care before hard work

As mentioned in the previous chapter, it is much easier to prepare a horse for a special day if he can be brought into a stable the night before. Presuming, then, that you *can* bring him in for a night, choose a stable which is well ventilated without being draughty and leave the top door open. Bed it down well and have a full haynet or rack ready (although the hay can be fed from the ground if the horse is a tidy eater) plus two buckets of water.

If it is winter and the horse normally wears a New Zealand rug outdoors you may be undecided as to whether to rug him up indoors or not. Be guided by the horse. If the base of his ears is cold, he feels cold and should have a single rug on. If you are going to clean him up, the rug will help keep him clean, anyway. If he feels warm, you could either leave him with nothing or just a light summer sheet, for cleanliness.

The horse should not be brought in wet and allowed to dry off on his own if the weather is at all chilly, especially with a winter coat. If you are going to wash him, do so quickly. Rub him down well with straw and/or old towels, and use a hairdryer if necessary. Finish him off by either thatching him with straw under an old rug or putting on an anti-sweat rug under an old top rug. Both these methods allow air to circulate between horse and rug and will keep him warm in cold weather whilst permitting him to dry off. Some horses' coats dry with the marks of the straw or mesh anti-sweat rug on them, but these marks can be removed or considerably lessened by removing the thatch and replacing with an ordinary rug to flatten the coat while the hair is still *very slightly* damp. The permeable rugs now available obviate the necessity for thatching as they allow moisture to rise up through them, and the horse dries off well.

Give the horse his normal corn feed, and check him again last thing to make sure he is not too hot from his unaccustomed accommodation. If he *is* too warm remove any clothing he is wearing but make sure there are no draughts. Next morning, visit him early to check on him, brush off any stable stains and feed and water normally.

Work on the day and aftercare

In winter, as he still has a good deal of his thick coat on, remember he will get hot much more easily than a clipped, stabled horse and cannot do the same amount of work. Do not do any more with him than necessary and do not let him stand about getting chilled. Keep him gently on the move and avoid any more energetic work such as fast cantering or jumping than needed, to minimise sweating as much as possible.

In summer, you will probably find that he performs just as well as a stabled or combined-system horse provided he is not too tubby from spring grass. If he starts to sweat or puff, obviously take things easy, stand him with his head to any breeze there might be and find a shady spot in hot weather.

On the way home, if hacking, your objective in both summer and winter is to arrive home with a cool, dry horse, weather permitting. With a horse wearing much or all of his winter coat, this may not be easy, but if it is pouring down with rain it is better to keep interspersing walk with steady trot to keep him warm, as a warm horse will dry off in his thick coat at home much quicker than a soaking wet, cold one. If boxing a wet horse home, remove the saddle and put on a permeable rug.

In summer, your task, once home, will be relatively easy. Even if it is raining and you feel tempted to let your horse spend another night indoors, don't. The weather is unlikely to be cold enough to cause him any distress and he will probably want to be out.

Whatever time of year it is, deal with the horse as quickly as possible to get him out again. In winter, use your common sense about drying off the horse. If he is wet with rain or sweat, but cool, he can go straight out in the field after a small feed. If he is warm, he must be cooled down by leading round, as to turn out a hot horse into a cold field on a winter night is asking for trouble. If it is raining and you cannot lead him round, put him in a cold stable or somewhere under cover and thatch him (or equivalent) or rub him down with straw until he shows signs of cooling down. Do not let him stand hot and sweating in a draught or in the open in the belief that he will dry off quicker. He will – but he will also probably get a chill. If the horse is to wear a New Zealand rug, he must, for reasons already stated, be dry before it is put on, so get him dry as quickly as possible while he is eating his feed, put the rug on and turn him out.

While your horse is eating his feed or hay, and maybe drying off, check him over for injuries and treat whatever you find. Obviously anything serious, deep cuts or lameness and the like, will need a vet's attention quickly, so the horse will have to stay in until help arrives, and instructions followed from then on. (If a horse has been kept in for several nights and/or days due to illness or injury, he will probably have to be stabled at nights for the rest of the winter as he will have become acclimatised to it, although if you are lucky enough to have a mild spell he would probably adapt once again to nights in the field if you keep a close eye on his reaction.)

Once the horse is out after his day's work, having had an initial feed, try to visit him later that night to check him and give him another feed. It goes without saying that his shelter should have its normal thick bed with hay supply and if he is having an extra feed because of his work, it may be necessary to feed him away from other field companions so that he gets his ration in peace.

The following day, the horse should be caught up and thoroughly checked over from head to hooves for any injuries not spotted the night before, for loose or cast shoes, and undue tiredness, and also trotted up to check for lameness. If he *is* injured or lame, he may have to be brought in to prevent his using the injured part too much in the field, so if you intend turning him out again, as detailed earlier, do not over-cosset him. Try to use a cool, airy stable with, in winter, as few rugs as are needed to keep him reasonably warm, and use your judgement about roughing him off again to return to his outdoor life when recovered.

Working straight from the field

When the horse is just being exercised normally or worked straight from the field without being brought in for a night, remember he will probably have been eating right up to the moment you go to catch him, so at least half an hour must be spent walking to let the grass go down before anything energetic can be undertaken. Normal exercise will take little out of a horse constantly on the move, and there is no need for specially cooked feeds (although outdoor horses, and indoor ones too, come to that, appreciate a warm feed on a cold night, just as we do).

It is often a nuisance to have a rain-wet horse when you want to ride and if the horse has a thick, muddy coat, too, it will not be possible to dry him off sufficiently to be able to get the saddle on if you have only limited time available. For this reason if no other, it is often a better plan to winter the horse out in a New Zealand rug and clip him a bit, than to have a horse who is constantly going to cause you to miss your rides because he is filthy or give you a lot of work cleaning him up. He will need the work anyway if you want him fit for fairly active work, so if the rug enables you to keep to a regular exercise/fitness programme, it is worth using.

In summer, I must admit to having frequently put a cotton fleece numnah on a wet but not muddy back, tacked up and got on with the riding. In this connection I do not see the difference between sweat and rain, and have never had any skin problems because of it. Rubbing mud into the back under the friction and weight of a saddle and rider would obviously be a different matter, and would make the skin sore quite quickly.

After moderate work in warm weather, the horse can have his normal feed (if he is getting concentrates) and be turned out as usual. If he is tired, it may be best to just put him out and let him eat the food which is easiest of all for him to digest – grass – giving him a normal feed later. This will get his digestion going again gently. Giving a tired horse, whether stabled or grass-kept, a full ordinary feed of concentrates is rather taxing to his tired system, and could cause colic as he may not be able to cope with it.

In winter, the grass will not be much use, so give him, say, a half feed perhaps with a carbohydrate booster in it as a quick energy restorative, with another later. After normal exercise, however, just give him his normal feed and put him back in the field as soon as practical.

Letting down whilst remaining at grass

If your horse has had a hard season's work, or you are unable, or do not want, to work him for a while, he can easily be let down for a rest simply by reducing his work over about a week. It is best to do this rather than stop possibly lengthy exercise or work stints all at once. Whether or not you reduce the feed, too, depends on the amount of grass available and on whether or not the weather is getting colder plus, as always, your horse's physical condition. Then, when you want to start work again, begin a fitness programme as normal.

Bringing up from grass

If you decide to bring your horse up from grass completely, try to do it gradually, as sudden changes of diet and way of life can be very upsetting. If the horse is not too fat, start by giving small concentrate feeds while he is still in the field, to begin a gradual changeover in diet if he has been having nothing but grass. If the horse has not been working, either, he can begin by having half an hour a day while still living out, just walking at first, of course. Even just riding him about his field, if he has no shoes on, will start to get his muscles working and his skin hardened up. This process could go on for a month or so, during which time you could call in the vet and the farrier to check over the horse's general condition, have teeth checked, feet seen to and shod, initially with lightweight shoes until the horse becomes accustomed to 'heavy' feet again, and generally get him going.

His grazing should be gradually reduced, not stopped all at once. No matter what anyone says to you, do *not* follow the old advice to 'mash the horse down', ie give sloppy mashes to 'convert' his digestive system from grass to hard feed. This will thoroughly upset his system and seriously unbalance the gut micro-organisms.

From starting work on an unfit, grass-kept horse to arriving at the end product of a fit, corn-fed, mainly stabled one, will take roughly twelve weeks. Over this period, very gradually reduce the grazing and increase the time stabled, until the horse is either being kept on the combined system or completely stabled, according to your requirements. There is never any need to completely cut out grazing for even the fittest horse. In fact, a daily ration of grass, even on the end of a leadrope for ten minutes, helps the digestion and will be relished by the horse.

After the first month or so of a fitness programme, you will start seeing a difference in the horse. During that first month, while you are gradually reducing the grazing and increasing the concentrates, the exercise should also be gently increased, until by the end of the month he could be receiving about an hour and a half a day mostly walking with perhaps a few minutes slow trotting. Concentrate rations depend on the individual horse, but he could now be getting about 2lb or 3lb (0.9–1.3kg) concentrates daily.

During the second month, build up the exercise to two hours a day, walking well up to the bridle rather than slopping along, with two ten-minute stints of steady trotting, using himself properly, and, towards the end of this month, short canter spells. His grazing by now can be cut to the minimum you have decided upon, and his droppings will have lost the green colour associated with those of a grass-kept horse and will be more khaki coloured and slightly firmer. Concentrates could be at about 6lb or 8lb (2.7–3.6kg) a day, always depending on the horse's requirements.

The final month of the fitness programme can be developed further, the horse being on a two-thirds bulk/one-third concentrate diet, or a little less bulk and more concentrates if doing fast work. More than two hours exercise will be unnecessary unless he is going in for endurance work, but grazing can still be given (provided it is not lush and over rich) for an hour or two a day with no harm to the horse.

If the horse is to be brought up from grass but not worked, the grazing should still be reduced gradually, and he will still need exercise of some sort unless sick, for the sake of his health. If he is to be yarded (kept in an area large enough for him to exercise himself but without grass) he should have a permanent supply of good hay or hayage, which alone could be enough to maintain his condition. Concentrates should be used as a top-up ration, in this case, to supplement the bulky diet if the horse appears to be on the thin side.

Should you be unable to reduce the grazing gradually for some reason, say if you suddenly lose the use of your field, graze the horse in hand anywhere convenient as much as you can and give him soaked hay or a hayage product with short feeds of whatever you were feeding in the field. If you were feeding nothing, start introducing small feeds of, say, molassed chop with soaked sugar beet pulp and grass meal. In cases like this where a digestive upset might easily occur, consider using a pro-biotic to help restore a healthy gut micro-organism population, and seek the advice of a nutritionist or vet. At present on the market is an excellent range of alfalfa (lucerne) products from Dengie which provide natural, balanced feeding regimes which could be ideal for your horse.

Turning out to grass

The process of turning a horse out to grass should be treated in the same way as that of getting a horse fit, although this reverse process does not take as long. The main point to watch is the weather; if the horse has wintered in and is being roughed off, and maybe let down, prior to turning out in spring, continuing cold weather can delay the process considerably. Just because the horse is now to be kept out (whether working or resting) it does not mean he can be expected to acclimatise himself within a week from an executive lifestyle, clipped, rugged up, stabled and corned up, to that of a camper, exposed largely to the weather, deprived of most of his rugs before his coat has grown and on a reduced corn/hay diet before the grass is making a respectable showing.

If the weather has warmed up, there is still a danger of adverse effects from a surfeit of rich spring grass, and if a horse is turned out in the autumn the weather could well be getting colder all the time he is being roughed off. It can take anything from ten days to three weeks or more to rough off a horse properly. The points to be borne in mind when working out a programme for it are:

1 The weather. Try to begin during a mild spell, especially if the horse has been clipped.
2 The horse's breeding and personal constitution.
3 How he has been kept (has he been turned out at all or not, is his stable cold and airy or warm and stuffy, how many rugs etc).
4 How much corn and exercise he has been getting. (If the horse is to remain in work these could stay the same.)

Let us assume the horse has wintered in and been 'chaser clipped (basically a trace clip with the head off, too), worked moderately (active hacking/light hunting) and has had short daily spells at grass. He is to become a working, outdoor horse.

The first thing to do is to worm the horse if this has not been done every few weeks throughout the winter, and get his teeth checked by the vet. Then, picking a mild spell, the first step in roughing off could be to start leaving the top leaf of his stable door open at night if it has been closed. Stop body brushing him to let the grease build up in his coat, but tidy him up with the dandy brush and attend to other items of his toilet as normal. As he is to stay in work, continue with feeding and exercising as normal, or cut down slightly. If the horse has been having about an hour a day grazing, double this time now. Continue like this for four days to a week.

The second stage involves leaving off one of his blankets, but only during the day if the weather is cold, and extending his time at grass to half a day, probably wearing a New Zealand rug. Everything else proceeds as before. Continue for about a further four days like this.

Thirdly, leave off a blanket at night and two in the day (if he has had two) so he stands in during the daytime with just his rug. He should now spend most of the day at grass when not working, with his 'mac' on, if chilly or wet. This stage could last four days again. Next, he should wear only a rug at night, nothing during the day when in and be out all day when not working, if possible without his New Zealand rug.

Finally, immediately prior to going out altogether, he should do without his stable rug completely. Pick a warmish night for his first night under the stars even though he has (it is hoped) a shelter and decide by assessing his progress and reaction to your programme whether to put his New Zealand rug on. This stage can be a little tricky as regards the rug. You might want to put it on only at night but find the horse is soaking wet from a day's rain, in which case he will have to be dried off first. Only you can decide if the horse is feeling cold, if he is tucked up and needing more food or if he has taken to the whole thing like a duck to water and is looking forward to his outdoor life, but I hope the above programme will give some idea of how to proceed when roughing off and turning out a horse.

Letting down a stabled horse

If the horse is to be let down from work and is going out for a rest, proceed as above, but also gradually cut down the exercise (by speed and duration) and concentrates. Eventually, if the grass is reasonable, cut down the hay ration too. If early spring, the horse could still need a feed or two a day, and possibly hay, too, if the grass is not properly through. In winter or autumn, although you can cut down the exercise, the weather may demand that his rations remain as when stabled. In summer, of course, it is hoped the grass will be enough to maintain a resting horse.

Acknowledgements

I am grateful for the help given in the preparation of this book by Mrs Marytavy Archer BSc DIC, Ms Janet L. Eley BVSc MRCVS and Mr and Mrs C. G. Taylor.

Index